CW01390603

WATER *from* ANOTHER TIME

TODAY'S QUESTIONS | YESTERDAY'S WISDOM

BERRY FRIESEN

SECOND EDITION

WATER *from* ANOTHER TIME

SECOND EDITION

COPYRIGHT © 2010
BERRY FRIESEN

All rights reserved.

Library of Congress Number: 2010914529
International Standard Book Number: 978-1-60126-252-3

Printed 2011 by
Masthof Press
219 Mill Road
Morgantown, PA 19543-9516
610-286-0258 | www.masthof.com

For our grandchildren,
Anna and Elena,
and all their cousins
of whatever degree.

*"The commandments of God
are to be remembered and taken to heart;
repeat them to your children
and speak of them both indoors and out-of-doors,
when you lie down and when you get up."*

Deuteronomy 6:6-7

Contents

"If we will only heed it, all the past is open to us, with its perilous seas and faerie lands forlorn, and we are free to set sail anytime we want. Our cultural myth is one of liberation, of the present breaking the shackles of the past. But what if it is the past that breaks the shackles of the present?"[1]
Frederick Turner

Preface

My interest in my family's story emerged after my mother died. That first winter, I spent many hours recording what I knew about her extended family and asking others to help fill the gaps in my knowledge. My wife, Sharon, often teased me by suggesting I enjoyed my dead relatives more than my living ones. I haven't had a ready answer to her jibe. What I have recognized in myself is a faintly desperate feeling that the stories of our families are slipping away and may soon be lost if I don't make a determined effort to retrieve them.

Of course, we each have the stories of our own lives to tell our children, as well as fragments we recall from the lives of our parents. Yet this volume is written with the assumption that to acquire the help we need from the past, we also need to acquaint ourselves with more distant ancestors and the contexts in which they made their choices.

Among 21st century Americans, it is assumed we give birth to ourselves through intelligence, skill and effort. While there is some truth in that assumption, my emphasis is on what we inherit – claimed or not – from the past. When we fully realize our potential, the gifts and consciousness that define us as individuals are brought into dialogue with the heritage we have received and the culture that formed us. That is the creative nexus, spiritually and otherwise. What I am trying to do with this book is provide enough information about our ancestors to enable at least some of my readers to reach that place.

Each era offers constraints as well as opportunities, blinders as well as new possibilities. In my lifetime, with the many advances in technology and more prosperous, cosmopolitan lives, we generally assume our lives are better than our ancestors' lives. But such an assessment is difficult to make within one's own time: our perspective is too limited. Certain worldviews have been closed to us; some paths to fulfillment and contentment have been blocked. We need help getting past our era's pervasive marketing, which often renders us incapable of even imagining a life different from what we have.

This is where history can help, even liberate us! Our ancestors embodied understandings of goodness and a life well-lived that will not occur to us unless we take the time to become acquainted with their stories. Once we do, new options open to us. Not all of those options will be attractive but we may find some to be life-giving.

Robert Inchausti calls this readiness to draw on moral and cultural resources from the past "a new form of traditionalism." It is, he writes:

> "[A] traditionalism that honors the old ways, not for their fascist energy or authoritarian solace, but for their revolutionary potential to throw off the yoke of an increasingly dehumanizing, mystifying and amnesic modern world. These new traditionalisms make possible an heroic response to existence . . . that is willful, dramatic, creative, and historically engaged, a response that tries to honor both the dead and the as yet unborn."

The danger in ignorance about our own social history, he writes, is not so much that we are condemned to repeat it but that we are left

> "unconscious to the larger drama of [our] own lives, morally and metaphysically diminished, trivialized and rendered irresponsible – cut off as it were from the sources of [our] own dignity."[2]

As I research the families that contributed to whom Sharon and I have become, I find myself wondering how my ancestors understood life. What did they think it was all about? In trying to answer that question, I have used interpretative categories of my own, categories that my ancestors may not have found useful. Be that as it may, from the outset I will be clear about what I see: highly religious families that also often displayed a political approach to life. Thus, along with the emphasis on

Christian teaching and practice, we find at many points the core elements of politically engaged people: group identity, public witness, and a struggle to achieve wider support for earthly goals. I invite readers to evaluate this for themselves.

Apart from worldviews, where do we begin the task of describing ancestors? Should we focus on the family line that carries our surname, even though that family line has contributed no more genetic material than dozens of others? Do we look back as far as possible to the earliest known ancestor, pretending there is something important about being first? Do we search for the most famous ancestor, pretending his/her fame reveals an essential quality of the family? Each approach seems arbitrary because we have been shaped by many different families.

My approach has been to start with Sharon and me and then tell stories from the families that contributed to who we are. To make that task manageable, I've paid most attention to the people in the three or four generations that preceded us. In general, these are the individuals who immigrated to the United States or were born here. The charts on pages 194 and 195 provide specific names and life-spans.

Just over half of the family names in those charts originated in the Low Countries and evidence our roots in 16th century Netherlands and Belgium.[3] All of the other names (von Riesen, Ratzlaff, Baltzer, Voth, Kroeker, Lohrentz, Funk and Rempel) became part of our family lines during the 250 years of life along the Vistula River (present day Poland). The sojourn in southern Russia (present day Ukraine) added no new names, nor did life in the United States during the 100 years between emigration from Russia and the birth of our daughters in the 1970s.

What this indicates is that the gene pool from which Sharon and I come has remained very shallow over the centuries. This reflects the social separatism that has characterized the Mennonites. More to the point of this writing, it suggests a cultural continuity through the generations. While I don't know much about more-distant ancestors, the consistency of their social and cultural milieu enables me to provide an outline of their lives.

Even after limiting through one method or another the number of ancestors considered, how does one describe multi-generational families? A chronological telling would be most helpful to the reader who wants to get acquainted with the cast of characters. But in families such as ours, comprised of simple folk who moved vast distances with some frequency and rarely gained the notice of anyone beyond their immediate circle, the historical record is skimpy and the gaps in chronology many.

So I have discarded any attempt to be chronological or comprehensive in my telling and have chosen instead to organize my material around five questions I regard to be timeless. Each question comprises a chapter, and each chapter collects stories that speak to the question at hand.

Such a structure will create difficulties for readers not acquainted with my context or family members. To reduce this difficulty and orient readers to my time and place, a brief autobiography follows this Preface.

I wrote this book to equip our daughters and their cousins to pass along to those who come after them an understanding of and appreciation for our heritage. But I am writing for others as well. From Sharon's and my parents and stretching back 400 years lays an unbroken line of people who were born into and shaped by faith-formed village life. Sharon and I were the first generation largely shaped by a more mixed environment and to grapple with the consequences of that diversity for ourselves and our children. Millions, no billions, have lived this transition. Sharon and I carry only the distinction of being rather late to join the crowds. But because we have been so late, we remain somewhat capable of reflecting on the before and after of it.

Each of us has a family and has been shaped by the unique features of that particular milieu. Yet those differences do not leave us moored in separate spaces. Indeed, we often develop perspective on our own experiences within family by listening in as other people reflect on theirs. This is what I hope readers from outside my family will experience when reading about the ordinary and unremarkable people described here.

As I write, my two brothers and their aptitudes for this task are on my mind. My oldest brother, LeRoy, has the insight and rigor to plumb the depths of our family's history. My second brother, Marley, had the detailed memory and story-telling ability to make history come alive. But I have aptitudes of my own. As the youngest of three, I watched my brothers from a distance, paying close attention to how they related to each other, our parents, and the world. From early on, LeRoy was a high achiever, drawing acclaim for the intelligence and passion he brought to various public endeavors. Early in his life, Marley had fewer public accomplishments but nevertheless drew quiet praise for his practical skills, amiability, and consensus-building approach. I deeply admired both brothers and tried to copy their more successful behaviors and attitudes. But because they were so different, following their examples was no simple task; it always seemed to involve choices I didn't want to make. And so I developed the habit of observing and evaluating, holding together things that tended to move apart. This is the deeply ingrained disposition and stance I bring to the writing of these stories.

Encouraging me on in my writing have been three friends who read early drafts: David Rempel Smucker, Glenn Lehman and Margaret High.

What follows, then, is what I have selected as most relevant from our families' stories to a few of what the inimitable Garrison Keillor calls "life's persistent questions." It is meant to be water from another time.[4] And like long-saved water priming a pump, the stories recounted here are meant to prompt reflection on what makes for a good life and how to live day-by-day with patience and hope.

Rainbow Hanger

Between hope and patience
stretches a short and hidden cord
binding each to the other
in quiet symbiosity.

Without hope, patience falters
leaving cynicism and wounded pride;
apathy follows
an alluring refuge of a barren kind.

And hope, apart from patience,
gazes ever upward for its end
towards realms of wishful thinking,
away from this our natural home.

Too rarely are we reminded
of the connection, abiding and deep,
between perseverance and recognition
of God's unequivocal assent.

Yet life itself poses the question--
when to act and when to rest?
keeps confronting our fevered spirits
with the discomfiting truth

that to believe in God almighty
rainbow hanger, stiller of seas
requires not zeal nor acquiescence
but stepping daily along the way.

---

[1] Turner, Frederick. "The Freedoms of the Past: On the Advantage of Looking Backward," *Harpers Magazine,* April 1995 at 59.

[2] Inchausti, Robert. *The Ignorant Perfection of Ordinary People,* State University of New York Press, 1991 at 3.

---

[3] Schreiber, William I. *The Fate of the Prussian Mennonites,* The Goettingen Research Committee, 1955 at 18-19.

[4] The phrase comes from a song of the same name written by folk-singer John McCutcheon. It speaks of the need for a mix of the new and the old. The metaphor "water from another time" comes from an era when hand pumps were used to bring water up out of a well. Such pumps depended on the suction created by the movement of a leather baffle within the pipe that reached down into the water. For the baffle to create a vacuum, it had to fit snugly against the walls of the pipe. And for it to fit snugly, it first had to swell after being made wet. The water at the bottom of the well was not accessible for this purpose. Thus, it was the practice to fill a small container with water and leave it near the pump. This water from another time would be poured over the baffle to moisten it, thus rendering it effective in bringing new water up from the bottom of the well. I sang McCutcheon's song to my granddaughter, Anna, at her first birthday party.

A Brief Autobiography

My father, John V. Friesen, began life in 1918 on a farm four miles north of the town of Fairbury in Jefferson County, Nebraska. He was the sixth child and the fifth son in a family that eventually grew to eight.

Dad's grandparents immigrated to the United States in 1874 and settled in Jefferson County. Their former homes had been in Russia (we now know it as the Ukraine), where they had been farmers. They immigrated along with a larger group of relatives and friends, most of whom were members of a Mennonite group called the *Kleine Gemeinde* or "little church." It was a close-knit and culturally separate group; some have described it as the "Amish faction" of the Russian Mennonites.

Dad's father was baptized by the *Kleine Gemeinde* congregation in Nebraska, but upon marriage joined the somewhat more progressive congregation his bride attended. Thus, Dad did not grow up with the severe social separatism that was his family's heritage.

My mother, Blondina Wiens, began life in 1918 on a farm in Cottonwood County, Minnesota. She was the fourth child and the first daughter in a family that eventually grew to eight. Her mother told her she had been named after a woman from long ago who had been martyred for her faith. I assume it was Blondina of Lyon, killed in 177 A.D. upon the order of the Roman emperor, Marcus Aurelius.

Mom was known as Blanche, a name she acquired from its frequent use in the romance novels she consumed as a teenager and even later in life. I always found it a point of pride to be the son of a woman named Blondina and known as Blanche. In the rural precinct we inhabited, it felt rather cosmopolitan. And it presaged my mother's idiosyncratic naming practices. She and Dad named their first-born LeeRoy, their second-born Marlyn and their third-born Berry. A few years after my birth, my name appeared in Mom's diaries as Barry; later, she reverted to the original spelling. Marlyn became Marly soon after his birth. Later, he borrowed an "e" from his older brother, after which they became Marley and LeRoy.

The Wiens family farm in 1918 was a 270 acre tract immediately east of the village of Delft. It included land Mom's grandparents had homesteaded after they immigrated in 1875. Their former homes also had been in Russia where they had been farmers. And like the Friesens, they immigrated as part of a larger group of relatives and friends who were Mennonites, albeit from a much larger and more progressive group.

In the summer of 1935, when Mom was 16, she met Dad while he was working on her uncle's farm, which adjoined her father's. They began to date and attended church services together. This upset Mom's father, who thought her too young to be in a romantic relationship. Dad sent Mom letters from Nebraska during the winters they were apart. That first winter, Mom's dad intercepted the letters and kept them from her. But the following summer, they renewed their romance and Mom's dad eventually came to accept the relationship. Mom and Dad married in September, 1939.

I was born in 1948, the last of three sons and nearly seven years after Marley, the brother closest to me in age. Mom had been counting on a girl, but visited none of her disappointment on me. As she wrote to me many years later, "It was all right that you were a boy instead of a girl." My parents had little material wealth when first married, but their economic situation had improved considerably by the time I arrived and I never suffered any sort of deprivation or awareness of material need. I enjoyed a very stable and happy childhood. From birth until my own marriage, I lived in the same place: the Balzer family farm my parents first occupied in 1945.

I met my future wife, Sharon Klassen, she with the twinkling eyes, as a small child in Sunday school. Beginning in 1952, her family of three girls and one boy began attending the same church my family attended in Delft. My first memories of Sharon are in grade school where Sharon and I were a grade apart. Our school had only two classrooms; grades 1-3 met in one room and grades 4-6 met in the other. By the time Sharon was in grade four and I in grade five, we were sweet on each other (we have the valentines to prove it). We began dating in the spring of 1964 when Sharon was in ninth grade. We had rough spots along the way, but kept an eye on each other and married in August, 1969.

Our marriage was the second involving the Klassen and Friesen families. Five years earlier, Sharon's sister, Mary, had married my brother, Marley.

In high school, I was a B+ student and that pattern continued at Tabor College, the Mennonite Brethren school in Hillsboro, Kansas I attended from 1966-1970. My skill as a basketball player and frequent leadership of student activities distinguished me in high school. In college, I continued to play basketball but gravitated more toward the edges of campus life where the social and religious conventions of my heritage were actively critiqued, questioned, and violated. Midnight during the off-season often found me at Leonidas' coffee shop in Newton, drinking coffee, smoking and talking with friends. I earned a "C" in my first calculus course, discovered I enjoyed the soft sciences more than the hard, and abandoned my plan of becoming an architect.

Tabor's first inter-term in the winter of 1968 brought Ed Riddick of the Southern Christian Leadership Conference to campus. He introduced me to the Civil Rights Movement. That March, along with seven other Tabor students, I attended a conference of the Intercollegiate (Mennonite) Peace Fellowship at Chicago's YMCA Hotel where speakers urged us to become advocates within our colleges, churches and families for black equality. "One speaker told us all hell is going to break loose unless America changes fast," I wrote in a letter to my parents. Days later, the Rev. Martin Luther King, Jr. was assassinated in Memphis, where he had been building support for the striking garbage workers. Across America, people took to the streets in anger. And I began to feel the first stirrings of something deep inside related to the importance of social and economic justice.

During my third year at Tabor, I took the winter semester on the campus of Wichita State University in a program called Cooperative Urban Teacher Education. It was an intensive education module designed to prepare secondary teachers from private Kansas colleges for urban and multi-ethnic classrooms. Local groups in the African-American community hosted many of our class seminars, I did my student teaching at the center-city high school (Wichita East), and that spring regularly worshiped with an African-American congregation.

I found the whole experience challenging but good and imagined I would secure employment in an urban high school after graduating. But the U.S. military drafted me in the spring of 1970, my last semester in college. In lieu of military service, I arranged a stipended assignment with Mennonite Central Committee (MCC) to teach junior high students in rural Glengoffe, Jamaica. It was a new school, built with funds from the World Bank, and part of the expansion of public education through grade nine (rather than ending after grade six). Although Sharon had not been drafted and still had a year left to finish her degree, she accepted an assignment like mine! In late July, we arrived in Kingston with five other MCC teachers. In this rather abrupt way, our college days ended, including most of the friendships we had formed during the years at Tabor. That first year, we felt intensely lonely.

Dad died early in our second year in Jamaica. It was harvest season in Minnesota and my parents were working together to move soybeans from a wagon to an overhead bin in the granary. Dad had been up in the granary, leveling the grain as the bin became full. After his descent, he collapsed on the ground beside the wagon Mom was tending. She found him immediately, but he was gone.

All of us had known of Dad's "heart condition" since he began to have chest pains in his late 30s. He had been overweight and addressed the problem by losing pounds and regularly taking a blood thinner. But the blockages within his cardiovascular system were never cleared and the chest pain continued. Though he remained active, he lived the last decade of his life with the awareness that another, perhaps fatal heart attack could strike at any time. I have vivid memories of some of those moments when he would stop in the midst of farm work and wait for the chest pain to ease. Here is what I wrote when I reached the age of 53, his age at the time of death.

In Memory of Dad

You'd pause to catch your breath
and let your heart recharge.
I'd stop, standing beside you
disconcerted by the look on your face
praying I'd know what to do
if you didn't stay on your feet.
Then, after a time,
we'd walk on over clodded soil.

I watched you as you learned to live
daily, with measured steps,
afraid of the uneven ground
yet courageous still;
stepping into uncertainty,
thoughts unbidden that
each could be your last.
You were what I understood a man to be.

Did you pause as you climbed into the granary head
to shovel the cascading grain?
Did you stop to calm your racing heart
before you descended out of the dust?
Back on solid ground,
did you pray as your vision began to narrow
and the earth began to tip
before you fell on that autumn day?

After we had completed our commitments in Jamaica, we returned to the Midwest in July 1973 to be close to family, especially my widowed mother. We lived one year in St. Cloud, Minnesota and then two years in Pocahontas, Iowa, where I taught high school social studies and coached boys' basketball.

In September 1976, I enrolled in the University of Minnesota's Law School, graduating in the spring of 1979. Our two children were born during that time – Amber during October 1976 and Emily during December 1978. After passing the bar exam, I practiced law for ten years with Southern Minnesota Regional Legal Services. During that time we lived first in St. Paul and later in Minneapolis, near our church.

In the spring of 1989, as part of my decision to accept a position at the headquarters of Mennonite Central Committee (MCC), we moved to Lancaster, Pennsylvania. I worked at MCC eight and one-half years. Since then, I have worked in Harrisburg with the Pennsylvania Hunger Action Center (1997-2008) and the Pennsylvania Health Access Network (2008-2009). Sharon has worked nearly our entire time in Pennsylvania as a paralegal with the firm of Russell, Krafft and Gruber in Lancaster.

Because of the structure of the book, some significant events receive little or no attention. One is my near-death experience in February 2000. I had just left the Lancaster train station after returning from a day's work when a blockage in a coronary artery caused my heart to stop. I collapsed on the sidewalk in front of the train station. A bystander called for emergency help; another began chest compressions to keep my blood circulating. A volunteer fire-fighter driving nearby heard the distress call on his radio and stopped to help. Two police officers responded to the call and used a defibrillator to shock my heart into motion again. An ambulance transported me to the emergency room.

Three days later, I regained consciousness as my family stood anxiously nearby. Their chief worry was brain damage that may have occurred during the minutes my blood was not circulating. Thankfully, aside from minor memory loss, I suffered no loss of function. This all would have ended differently had I been on the other side of the street from the train station, out of the public eye, when I collapsed. And it all would have ended differently but for the kindness of strangers.

Near death experiences often are described as life-changing. Others can better report than I whether such is the case for me, but I don't perceive it so. I continue to be afraid when I imagine death may be near. I continue to forget God's faithfulness and become anxious when life doesn't go well for me or my loved ones. Gratitude, which by rights should saturate my life, often shows up only after being prompted. Yet the experience also has marked me in ways I can't readily identify. Perhaps writing this book is one of them; I know how quickly this wonder called life can end.

When we left Minnesota, we expected to return. Indeed, just prior to our discovery that Mom was suffering from bone marrow cancer, we were making plans to do just that. But after her death in November, 1996, we didn't feel the same urgency to return. Sharon's father had died earlier that same year from complications related to congestive heart failure, and although Sharon's mother needed support, oldest sister Evangeline (Vangie) was a nurse and lived nearby. After nearly a decade in Pennsylvania, our daughters were well-rooted, so we have not moved back to the place of our origins. Lancaster has become our home.

Here is a poem celebrating my nearly life-long relationship with Sharon. It was written in 2006 around our 37th wedding anniversary.

Anniversary

We've walked this way together
for half a lifetime now, even more
if we count the courting,
you close beside me in your summer dresses
caressing my head with your open hand.

Since then, seems we've faced mostly
into the wind, stumbling some
but never falling headlong,
focused on a promise we see best
through tearing eyes.

It's bracing, this journey together
our steps side-by-side,
I turning toward the rushing air
you keeping steps and space between us
in counterpoint harmony.

Now, our path has taken us here -
an unremarkable couple in an ordinary place
with flowers in the yard and bills to pay,
faces creased from squinting
knees soon in need of repair.

Still, being close to you brings me pleasure
unlike the beginning yet somehow the same.
Still, our walking makes us stronger,
looking ahead
knowing God meets us there.

"Make a home.
Help to make a community.
Be loyal to what you have made." [1]
Wendell Berry

Chapter 1: Where will we live?

The world has many fine places to live, each offering opportunities as well as challenges. How does one decide where to call home? And how does one decide to leave one home for another? Our families often have dealt with these questions, sometimes reluctantly and sometimes with great anticipation.

California Dreaming

In the Minnesota farm home where I grew up, my parents frequently talked about California. Three of Dad's four brothers and one of his two sisters lived there, and every couple of years, they visited us or my parents visited them.

Dad first visited California in 1937 on a 5,000 mile road trip with his parents and a younger brother and sister. They visited Helena, the sister who lived in Washington, drove portions of the newly-completed Pacific highway as they came south, and spent time with Henry, the brother who lived near Fresno. A decade later, married and the father of two little boys, Dad took his family to California for a visit. They traveled from Minnesota in a ten-year-old Chevy, which broke down near Ogallala, Nebraska on the first day of their trip. On the fifth day, they scaled Donner Pass and then descended toward Reedley, where Dad's relatives lived. They settled in for five weeks, enjoying the indoor plumbing and the hospitality of extended family. Soon after returning to the January cold of Minnesota, Dad began to remodel the kitchen pantry into an indoor bathroom. The days of the chamber pot were over; California had shown a better way!

Dad and Mom made five or six more trips like that during the '50s and '60s. Dad loved each one; he was fond of his siblings and California's many sights. And he dreamed of living and prospering there in the San Joaquin Valley, along with Aunt Lena, Uncle Henry, Uncle Herman, and Uncle Jack. After a trip west over the Christmas of 1963, Dad got serious about moving. An auto dealer in Fresno had offered him a sales position; this was the opportunity Dad had been waiting for.

For a few weeks in the dead of winter, talk of sunny California charged our days. Dad was enthusiastic and Mom reluctant, at least in the conversations I heard. She enjoyed their home on the farm where her great-grandparents had settled after emigrating from Russia. She felt loyal to her church. There was her elderly mother to think of and a brother, Harold, who lived just a mile down the road. Then there was the glamour and newness of California, which she had never appreciated much. Whether the final decision turned on Mom's reluctance or some other factor, I never knew. But the conversations dwindled and we stayed on the farm in Minnesota.

For me, the experience revealed an insight about my father: he wanted to live somewhere else. His private dreams of life as he hoped it could be took him to a place far from our lovely Minnesota farm.

The Klassens[2] Settle In

The Klassen branch of Sharon's ancestors arrived in the United States (specifically, Philadelphia harbor) on July 25, 1875 after crossing the Atlantic Ocean from Antwerp. About 450 Mennonite immigrants, all from south Russia, were on board. Their party included Sharon's great-great-grandparents, Gerhard and Maria, both in their early fifties; married son Gerhard (his wife and two children came a year later); unmarried children, Peter and Anna; daughter Maria and her husband Johann Friesen; and son Abraham and his wife Elizabeth Voth. Each of the two couples had three children so the Klassen family group numbered fifteen in all.

The oldest member of their party, Elizabeth's mother, died during the crossing. The ship's crew buried her body by lowering it into the sea.

In Philadelphia, the Klassens boarded a train and headed west to Chicago, then on to St. Paul, and finally to a new village on the prairie of southwestern Minnesota. U.S military forces had expelled the Santee people (also know as the Dakota Sioux Indians) from that corner of the state in a five-week war during 1862. Railroad building commenced a few years later. The village that was the Klassens' final destination had been established in 1872 about midway between Sioux City and St. Paul, the endpoints of the new rail line. Two miles southeast of the rail station was a large, shallow lake with a prominent island at the center. In a moment of grandiosity, the town fathers dropped the name Midway and instead called the place Mountain Lake.

H.E. Wiens, a son of one of those early immigrants, described what it was like to get started.

> "The first problem that they faced was to find a home for their families and to earn their bread and butter. Some were fortunate to buy a small house from a previous homesteader of the land. Most of the newcomers, however, bought an open tract of land and quickly constructed a simple house of sods or clay bricks, with hay-thatched roofs. Heavy rains often caused the clay brick to crumble away and the work had to be done over." [3]

For many, the first few years in Minnesota were very discouraging. Here are the recollections of John J. Becker, a boy of eight at the time.

> "There were many disappointment and trials, and many heavy sighs of soul searching and prayers to God for relief. In those hours their thoughts returned to the home they had left and their hearts were filled with sadness and longing as they remembered those who had remained behind. And many a one would have taken up his walking stick and returned to his own home if only he had the money. But they had to stay and acquire fresh courage.
>
> "But how much had been left behind? A beautiful home within a beautiful settlement with much beautiful furniture, which provided for them an economical, social, spiritual and ecclesiastical regime. Economically they had beautiful farms and beautiful buildings, well planted orchards and pastures.

"In comparison, here we have inconspicuous farms scattered in the middle of a wild prairie, small sod huts, straw barns, no orchards. This change was no small matter and required much work, expense and time in trying to bring our condition, in some measure, like the old home we had left behind. This also set our economy very far back. But even worse were the social amenities. Back in our former homeland, in close-knit villages, with our farm yards next to each other, there were pleasant opportunities for socializing. And especially when there was sickness or an accident, help was always nearby. In contrast, here with these scattered farms, socializing and help in time of sickness or accident is very difficult. Another loss is felt in trying to overcome discouragement."[4]

The Klassens arrived during the third year of a five-year plague of grasshoppers that devoured nearly all crops and vegetation, devastating the economic prospects of farmers already settled there. Some had given up and began selling tracts of land with existing buildings and other improvements at bargain prices. Gerhard and Maria took advantage of that opportunity. On August 14, they purchased 160 acres in the northeast quarter of Section 28 of Mountain Lake Township for $2,550, which worked out to just under $16 an acre. (The tract was four miles straight south of town and at the southwest corner where the Windom road intersects.) The land had been homesteaded and improved by the previous owners and we can be reasonably certain it already included a house and barn. Over time, one or two additional residences were built on the property and the Klassens' youngest daughter, Anna, lived there with her husband after they married in 1878.

Sharon great-grandparents, Abraham and Elizabeth Klassen, acquired their property via the homestead process. It was an 80-acre tract one-half mile east of Gerhard and Maria, along the southern edge of Section 22. Most of the work that first autumn probably focused on the construction of simple shelters on that property, which was virgin prairie with no trees or buildings of any kind.

The Klassen family suffered much during those early years. In 1877, son Gerhard died of unknown causes at age 32, leaving a widow and two young children. Son Abraham died in the spring of 1880 at age 28, again of unknown causes. He left his wife, Elizabeth, and five young children. The next day, Elizabeth gave birth to her sixth. Abraham, the eldest child, was just eight years old at the time of his father's death.

After burying her husband in the graveyard along the west edge of Section 22, Elizabeth took her children and the few head of livestock she owned and moved in with her parents-in-law. She lived with them a year. During that time, she became better acquainted with Heinrich Flaming, a bachelor farmer who owned the land just north of Elizabeth's acreage. They married in April, 1881 and then moved into the home Elizabeth and Abraham had built during the five years they had lived together in Minnesota. Flaming had a bit of money (he bought shoes for all of the Klassen children to wear at the wedding), was a good provider and raised the six Klassen children as his own. With him, Elizabeth had five additional children, the last in 1893.

Apart from her roles as homesteader, spouse and mother, Elizabeth was a midwife. She had received some obstetrics training in Russia and continued to train with physicians in the Mountain Lake area. During her 40 years of midwifery in Minnesota, Elizabeth helped pregnant women bring 2,000 babies into the world (about one each week). She often was away from her home and family because of this work. In 1902, the Minnesota State Board of Medical Examiners certified her for the practice of midwifery. She passed along her knowledge and skill to her oldest daughter, Helena, who also became a midwife, practicing primarily in Montana.

As a young man, Elizabeth's oldest son, Abraham, used his skills in carpentry and woodworking to earn a living. In January 1899, when he was 26, Abraham married 17-year-old Justina Wiebe, a neighbor girl who lived on the opposite side of the section, They moved into a new house Abraham built as a wedding gift for his bride; it was located at the west end of Mountain Lake along the highway running through town. Their first child, also named Abraham, was born nine months later. Through the years, eight more children arrived and all were raised in that house on the highway.

In 1920, when Abraham was 48, the H.P Goertz Lumber Company appointed him general manager of its Mt. Lake yard. He performed this role for 22 years, helping area farmers and businessmen plan building projects and then selling them the required construction materials. One of his retirement projects was very prominent early in my life: the Carson Mennonite Brethren Church, built 1948 in Delft.

Abraham was an artisan, specializing in wood-inlay on tables and in framed wall compositions. His creations sold briskly at the annual July 4th Mission Sale. He donated his finest piece, a portrayal of the Lord's

Supper, to the Mountain Lake Eventide (Senior) Home. Several of his tables and wall displays remain among his Klassen descendants.

His children remembered him as generous and good-humored, a father who enjoyed them and often treated them to candy, ice cream and rides in his car. Youngest daughter Amanda wrote in 1977:

> "Next to all the candy Pa brought me or gave money [to buy], was the two play houses he made us. First that little one, then the big one and all the furniture to go in it! We got first prize on a Pow Wow [Mountain Lake's annual June festival] float. [My brothers] Sam and Bill helped him. They put it on the lumberyard truck, extended it with boards and put a big apple tree branch on it. [It] looked like a front lawn in front of the house. As we drove thru town, [my sister] Elizabeth and I sat on little chairs with our dolls. We have a picture of it. He made us two little cupboards; one was painted white, the other was bigger and was varnished. He also made us a round table and glued a picture on it and then varnished over it and we had chairs to go with it and tiny benches too. . . . Pa made us many nice things and we loved [him] so for doing it."
>
> . . . .
>
> "One time when I was little, I was sitting at the table and playing with paper dolls, made from a catalog, and Pa came and sat down next to me and just grinned – that special grin I liked so. He didn't say a word and then gave me a kiss; his mustache was shaved off!"

As best we can reconstruct family life, Justina was in charge at home, setting the tone, "keeping house," and teaching the children the ways of Jesus. Here again are Amanda's recollections.

> "What I loved more than anything in all my childhood and youth was that now and then, Ma took me along into her bedroom and asked, 'Is there something special we can pray about together?' And we did! We talked, we prayed and I cried. It meant ever so much to me!"

As Amanda remembered it, during the Depression years, their mother's responsibilities included hosting unexpected guests.

"I often think of the many hoboes who came regularly to our home in summer. Some slept up on the hay loft in the barn/garage. One guy came many summers and we got to know him and almost trust him too. I wasn't sure what to think of it when we saw some of the bums mark that one front tree as they left. We thought it was a marker for the next time around or maybe a clue for the next bum. Ha! But the good part was when these train hoboes came and asked for food, Ma could never refuse them. She would ask them to be seated on the porch and she went inside to prepare food. I watched it with great interest, standing closer to Ma than the dirty guys. Then while they eagerly ate, Ma sat down and 'preached' to them. She told them that Jesus loved them and always asked them, 'Have you been in contact with your mother lately? Have you written to her recently?' She demanded an answer and they couldn't leave until they promised her that they would write to their mother."

William entered this family in 1911 as the sixth child. He grew up on the west side of town, played basketball and tennis in high school, and graduated in 1929. After a year of junior college in Independence, Kansas, he enrolled at the University of Minnesota to prepare to study medicine. But by the age of 20, he was back in Mountain Lake working for his father at the lumber yard. At age 21, after a spiritual awakening, he requested membership in the Mennonite Brethren Church and was baptized in August of 1932. In that congregation, he met Esther Eytzen; they married in 1938. And like his father, William built his bride a new house in Mountain Lake, on Second Avenue, near the Lutheran church.

By 1942, Will (or Bill as he was known around town) had succeeded his father as general manager of the lumber yard, now owned by W.E. Thomas Lumber. Ten years later, he and Esther went into business for themselves through the purchase of the Strunk lumber business in Delft, an unincorporated village of about 100 people eleven miles northwest of Mountain Lake. They financed the purchase with their own savings and the investment of a sister and brother-in-law, Justina and Lee Janzen, who lived in California. Will managed the building trade and Esther the financial records. To facilitate these new responsibilities, the entire family – now including four children – moved to Delft and became part of the life of that village.

Most of their business trade involved area farmers who needed building materials for the upkeep and expansion of their barns, sheds and houses. During the late '50s and early '60s, many farmers began to participate in a plan that enabled them to hold their grain off the market and receive storage payments from the U.S. Department of Agriculture. To participate, farmers needed additional storage capacity and Klassen Lumber filled that need by designing and constructing movable grain bins built on skids with frame walls and pitched roofs. The dimensions varied, but a typical storage building was 14 feet by 24 feet. Will sold many of these bins to area farmers.

During the early 1960s, through his association with a national firm that sold building materials, Will introduced pre-fabricated roof trusses to Cottonwood County. Employees built the trusses in the lumberyard according to engineered specifications using dimension lumber and metal nailing plates called "gang-nails". The early fabrication process involved pounding the nailing plates into the wood using a heavy vehicle axel as a hammer. It was not work the human body could long endure and as the orders piled up, so did employee complaints.

In early 1965, Will and Esther purchased the Thomas Lumber yard and business in Mountain Lake, installed a hydraulic press, and moved the truss assembly operation there. This enabled the business to fill truss orders required by farmers building long barns for turkeys and chickens. Many of the barns built across the County during this era included Klassen Lumber Yard trusses.

At about the same time, Will and Esther bought the lumber yard in Jeffers. But the Mountain Lake yard was the key to their operation and so in 1965 they moved back to Mountain Lake to directly manage that facility. The Delft and Jeffers yards were sold after a few years; the Mountain Lake yard continued under Will and Esther's control until 1978, when they sold it to daughters Vangie and Mary and their husbands, Ron Patrick and Marlyn Friesen. They operated the business as partners until 1984 when Vangie and Ron sold their share and used the money to start a restaurant.

*****

My brother, Marley, died on a cold February Sunday in 1986. He had just loaded a sheet of plywood into the back of his pick-up truck and had climbed behind the steering wheel. Something about the asymmetric motion of wrestling with that sheet of plywood sent his heart into a quivering motion. He died there a few days short of his 44th birthday, his foot pushing against the accelerator, the motor roaring.

We had known for a couple of years that Marley had a cardiac problem known as hypertrophic cardiomyopathy (also known as IHSS). It was a congenital condition that emerged fully during his late thirties, thickening the middle wall of his heart and compromising its capacity to pump blood efficiently. In his late thirties, LeRoy developed the same condition. We later discovered it had been passed to them by our mother, who apparently received it from her father. In retrospect, Uncle Ted Wiens' early death at age 42 and Great-uncle Abraham Wiens' death at age 30 also are attributable to this genetic defect.

With Marley's passing, Mary carried on alone what the two of them had done together, including the operation of the lumber business. Sons John and Ben, 14 and 10 at the time of their dad's death, helped where they could.

Those were difficult economic times in rural Minnesota. Rising farm land values during the late 1970s and early 1980s had led to liberal credit arrangements and a boom in land acquisitions and improvements. But when land values stopped rising, banks started demanding loan repayment out of farming operations. Many farmers could not meet the new requirements. Starting in 1984, a wave of foreclosures rolled across the countryside. By 1986, many Mountain Lake area farmers had hunkered down, fighting off the lenders and trying to survive by restructuring their farm operations. They had no money available for building improvements. Business at the lumber yard slowed to a trickle.

Mary's father stepped back into the business after Marley's death in the hope that his skill in planning and estimating jobs would increase sales. It helped a little, but the undertow of the depressed economy was too strong. In late 1987, after a year and one-half of solo management, Mary sold the business to the local agricultural cooperative. Basically, it was an inventory sale and she received nothing for the reputation of the business and the years of building relationships with area customers.

Now what? Still in her early forties, Mary needed to make a living and provide for her two sons. In 1989, after John graduated from high school, the family moved to Minneapolis and started over. John enrolled in Bethel College in Kansas, Ben enrolled in Minnehaha Academy, and Mary secured employment in the Academy's office. A year later, she began managing the Jubilee Shop, an alternative trade gift store that was part of the Ten Thousand Villages retail network. Mary managed the shop for seven years and until her 1997 marriage to Delbert Seitz, a widower from Harrisonburg, Virginia. After their marriage, they made their home first in Harrisonburg and later in Lancaster, Pennsylvania.

*****

Imagine a fine hotel linked to a surgery center. A place to receive state-of-the-art medical care while one's family and loved ones are nearby to lend emotional support. Yes, the sort of facilities one finds at the Mayo Clinic. In 1928, a physician and surgeon named Harvey Basinger created this reality in Mountain Lake. He built a four-story building at the center of town; it had a surgery center on the top floor and hotel facilities (including a restaurant and meeting rooms) on the lower three floors. It was a Minnesota landmark.

Thirty years later, after serving many ill patients and their families, the facility closed as other locations eclipsed Mountain Lake as centers for medical care. The hotel and surgery center sat empty for a time, was converted for a time into a nursing home, and then sat empty again.

Vangie and Ron saw the building's potential. At a time when Mountain Lake's main street businesses were shutting down, they acquired the vacant building with the leaking roof and opened a restaurant in the former hotel coffee shop. Gradually, over a period of years, they renovated the upper floors into apartments, occupying the first one themselves.[5] In the fall of 1994, Vangie's parents, Esther and Will Klassen, occupied another apartment, just across the hall.

Early in 1996, Will died due to congestive heart failure. Esther, 81 years old and in chronic pain from arthritis and a childhood back injury, became a widow. She expected her remaining time would be short but she lived another thirteen and one-half years.

Can an elderly individual with chronic pain live independently? Esther did. She maintained her own home there until the day she died at age 94, welcoming the extended family when it gathered and occasionally hosting dinners at her table as well as in the restaurant below. Supported by Vangie's and Ron's vision and their presence just across the hall, Esther continued there on Main Street until the very end.

As Sharon's mother, Esther has long been important to me. Over time, I came to appreciate her not only for the wonderful daughter she raised but also for her contributions directly to my life. Some of this I described in this poem, read to her at her 90th birthday party.

To Esther

When I was young you were my sweetheart's mother,
the one whose instruction she revered,
whose influence thwarted my fondest dreams.

Then, when the bright flame of love continued,
you welcomed me into your family –
setting aside reservations you held deep inside.

No sooner had I claimed your youngest daughter
when far from you we flew. Little did I know
the ache that brought into your heart.

Later still, when your granddaughters lived in my house,
I asked your blessing to leave yet again.
Approval and empowerment, one generation to the next,

this – and more -- you gave in a spirit generous and wise,
confident always it is God who writes the part of the story
that will be remembered at the end.

This portion of the Klassen family's story covers 135 years in and around one community. It includes the operation of area businesses; membership in local congregations, civic associations, and the hospital board; attendance at local schools; and the gifts of neighborliness and friendship. The Klassens made a home, helped to make a community, and stayed loyal to what they had made. It is a record worthy of praise.

My Country Home

The farm where I grew up consisted of a set of buildings, 80 acres owned by my parents, and 120 acres rented from the previous owner, a relative named Abe Balzer. The buildings sat near the middle of Carson Township's Section 29, atop a gentle rise. The house looked east toward the rising sun and could be clearly seen from the main road. To the west and north of the farm yard stood two rows of mature willow trees, a barrier against winter wind and snow. As one approached on the long driveway, the trees framed and sheltered the activity in the farm yard.

Mom's Balzer ancestors had been the first to farm there and during the first decade of the 20th century had constructed the buildings my parents and brothers first occupied in the fall of 1945. The house looked similar to others in the area and was nothing special: two stories, four small bedrooms upstairs and one down, built in two sections that joined each other at right angles, making the roof ridges into a perfect T. Mostly, we lived in the large kitchen.

Outside, on the other hand, was special! It included a garden, an apple and plum orchard, an empty space for us brothers to play softball, and another for everyone to play croquet and badminton. A bit further a-field, there was shaded pasture between the rows of willows. LeRoy and Marley built wooden clubs to play golf there one summer; during another, they built a tree-house. Some summer afternoons when I was a boy, Mom would pack a lunch of dried apples, raisins and oatmeal cookies and we'd wile away the time in the meadow under the willows.

The barn had two levels, the upper part, the mow, filled with straw for bedding the livestock and hay for their feed. On winter days that weren't too cold, it was the perfect place to play: quiet, far from adults, and largely at our disposal. We could arrange the bales any way we pleased, so long as we didn't break them apart. And arrange we did, into a maze of forts and tunnels that fueled our fantasies for hours.

The machine shed included a workbench, Dad's tools, and a generous assortment of bits and pieces that we assembled into whatever caught our fancy. I made model airplanes and rifles out of wood, repainted my bicycle, dissembled and successfully reassembled an old lawnmower engine. Marley made a toy-set of road-building equipment there one spring. After adding my Christmas toys, we had everything we needed to build dandy highways through and around the sandbox under the big tree behind our house.

Life on the farm was dictated by the seasons. During the winter, coping with the cold and the deep drifts of snow occupied our attention. It was mundane activity, yet it touched on matters of basic survival: keep the pipes unthawed so the animals can get water, fill the feed troughs, make sure the cars and tractors start, push the snow off the driveway so we can get to church, school and the grocery store.

Then, before winter was really over, we'd have new lambs to tend, sometimes late into the night. And soon after, we'd receive hundreds of fragile, baby chicks that would be dead by morning if the propane-lit fire in the cone-shaped brooder stoves went out.

Spring was the season when lightning strikes and crashing thunderstorms sent us scurrying for cover. Between the rains, we'd start the field work. That always involved another harvest of rocks the winter cold had pushed to the surface. The soil itself needed to be tilled and prepared for the seed. Dad planted the fields, Mom and I the garden.

In summer, we lived nearly every day out in the sun and the wind, cultivating the row-crops, baling hay, and walking through the soybean fields in search of thistles and cockleburs. We'd break for dinner at noon, washing off the grime with Lava soap and cold water over a tin basin in the back entry to the house, drying ourselves with a feed sack that hung from a nail. We'd break again for afternoon lunch; supper waited until the day's work was done.

With luck, fall was the best of all, especially if it included a bountiful harvest and happy adults all around. Everyone had a job; all hands were needed. Once the harvest began, meals were served in the fields out of picnic baskets; we sat on whatever we could find (often our haunches) and ate our fill. We'd work late into the night, sometimes under a big yellow moon. We felt like adults, long before we were grown, because we each played a part in bringing in the harvest, work that has sustained life since time began.

Finally, with harvest season behind us, the work would nearly stop. The chores with the animals would continue, as would our trips outside to fetch corn cobs for burning in the kitchen stove. But by and large, we'd stay inside, enjoying the big, warm kitchen and using the flush toilet again. There we'd prepare for Christmas and wait for the spring.

*****

The farm was an idyllic place to grow up, yet my brothers and I always intended to leave. None of us seriously considered returning to the farm to live, whether as a farmer or in some other livelihood.

It was much the same in Sharon's family. Notwithstanding its long history in the Mountain Lake area, she and her siblings also grew up with the expectation they would live as adults somewhere else.

Where did this come from? Perhaps it reflected the view that our community was a backwater, far from urban vitality, provincial in its outlook and stunted in its opportunities. Only those without ambition or talent could thrive in such a small world, we seemed to assume. Not wanting to think of ourselves as deficient in spirit or ability, we committed early to being among those who would leave.

Partly our expectations grew out of the value our parents placed on higher education. Although they had little education themselves (only Sharon's father had finished high school), they wanted us to get college degrees so we'd have access to a range of livelihoods.

Another factor propelling us outward was the Christian idealism our churches gave us. "Go ye into all the world and preach the gospel," Jesus had told his disciples as he was about to leave them. The congregation we grew up in taught us this was our responsibility too.

True, most of us felt no call to be preachers or missionaries, but we did intend to let our light shine wherever we lived. Like Joseph in Egypt and Esther and Daniel in Iran, our humble roots could not obscure the sincerity of our intentions, the honesty of our words, and the top-notch quality of our work. The world welcomed dependable people, our church assured us; God would bless us with success.

Given the long rural tradition and closed communities from which we came, one might have expected our elders to challenge shallow optimism about how we would impact the world for Christ (and teach it a thing or two about honesty and quality work). But that didn't happen, perhaps because such realism had already been sloughed off in exchange for a success-oriented attitude in which our religious faith served as our secret asset. Get a college education and then proceed with one's chosen career in a manner that reflects the ethics and beliefs of a born-again Christian; that was the roadmap I recall being given.

Growing up, I generally accepted my congregation's guidance in this regard. There was plenty of evidence that it worked. The Mennonite Brethren congregations of Cottonwood County had sent many highly successful people into the world;[6] I could be one of them.

My second thoughts only began during the three years Sharon and I lived in Jamaica. There we developed deep respect for our uneducated friends and neighbors. The village where we lived, Glengoffe, was so far off the beaten track that we had sufficient time and distance to develop a critique of the materialism and go-go lifestyle of North Americans. When we returned to Mountain Lake and the farm in the summer of 1973, I recall thinking for the first time that it would be a good place to live. But somehow, the idea didn't stick.

A year later, in the summer of 1974, Vangie and Ron moved from Aurora, Illinois back to Mountain Lake. I was surprised; this was like water running uphill. People left Mountain Lake; they didn't return to it. I resolved the dissonance by speculating that Vangie and Ron's prospects in Illinois had not been so promising. Two years later, when Mom put the 10-acre farm building site up for sale to fund the construction of a new house in Mountain Lake, we expressed no interest in purchasing the place where a branch of our family had lived for nearly 100 years. Instead, we wanted to engage the wider world.

In 1978, I had a second surprise. Mary and Marley decided to move from the western suburbs of Minneapolis to Mountain Lake to buy into the Klassen Lumber Yard. I was sufficiently acquainted with their lives to know their move had nothing to do with poor prospects. They were seeking opportunities they didn't have in the city: own their own business, participate in the shaping of their own community, and weave lasting relationships across three generations.

Obviously, some re-evaluation was underway within our family about the merits of the home community. But by then, I was a law student and Sharon and I felt committed to living in more urban settings. Though we had fleeting thoughts over the years of returning to Mountain Lake, we never made a serious attempt.

******

I can't say I believe in sacred places, where the spirit of God is especially close to us and more accessible to our senses. But some places remind us of people whose commitments sanctified the space where they lived, loved and labored.

Rat Lake is such a place for me. It is small and shallow, nearly filled with marsh grass and cattails, and lying almost entirely in section 20 of Carson Township. Dad taught me to fish for bullheads there one spring day many years ago. Later, I hunted there with my boyhood friend, Gene Bartsch, for pintails, mallards, and canvasback ducks. Sharon's brother, Paul, trapped muskrats there during the winters of his teenage years, harvesting the pelts as a source of spending money. Years later, on a trip back from Pennsylvania, it's where I first saw a Northern Waterthrush, a Great White Pelican, a Black Tern, and a Common Goldeneye.

Near the western edge of the lake, about halfway across the section, my great-grandparents, Jacob and Maria Balzer, built their first home after marrying in 1883.

To the north is the site where they built a second wood frame house and barn for their family during those first years of the 20th century. As a boy, I played there while my mother canned garden produce with Aunt Lizzie Balzer. Just a little north and west of the lake is the tract great-grandfather Wiens homesteaded, the house Grandpa built when Mom was a teenager, and the graves where Dad and Mom are buried.

To the east is land farmed during my youth by Uncle Harold and Aunt Helen Wiens. They often hired me to help with haymaking and corn cultivation, and I remember pausing to eat mulberries as I drove the tractor beneath the trees along the fence between their land and the lakeside pasture.

To the south lies the farm settled by the Voth family, where Rev. Heinrich Voth had his little German School each winter. There he lived with his two youngest sons before sending them in the dark of night to Canada, far from the reach of the U.S. government and orders to kill Prussian soldiers in President Wilson's "war to end all wars."

All this history and much more lies in the two-mile space between the farm where I was raised and the village of Delft where Sharon was raised. By rights, it should be called Balzer Lake, after those who first settled around it. But maybe Rat Lake is the right name. After all, the Balzers came and went while the muskrats have endured.

Sometimes I wish I had too.

Starting in the Low Countries

Our families acquired much of their identity and character in West Prussia (Poland today), where ancestors lived along both banks of the Vistula River. That is where they acquired a common language, *Plautdietsch,* and our ethnic identity as Mennonites. That period – roughly 250 years between 1550 and 1800 - is by far the longest period family members ever lived in one place.

We can be confident of tracing the family's story even further back. One of Sharon's family lines, through her grandmother Justina, is confirmed back to 1521 in the person of Jan deVeer, born in the Dutch province of Zealand. His son, Gysbert Jansz deVeer, was born in South Holland, was baptized in Amsterdam, and became a grain merchant in Danzig after his marriage to Debora Claesdochter Harnasveger.[7] Two of my family lines (through Margaretha Wiebe, who married Abraham von Riesen in 1779, and through Margaretha Matthies, who married Johann Wiens in 1776) go back to the same deVeer and Harnasveger families.

Beyond this distant root, our families' histories have a predominance of Low Country names, including Wiens, Dueck, Klassen, Flaming, Wiebe, Eytzen, Enns, Harms, Reimer, Goertzen and Janzen.

Why are there so many Low Country names? And how did those families get transplanted in eastern Europe?

To fully answer these questions, we would need to refresh our knowledge of the Protestant Reformation that swept across Europe during the years after Martin Luther nailed his *Ninety-Five Theses* on the Wittenberg cathedral door in 1517. It precipitated far-reaching religious and social changes in Belgium and the Netherlands and a violent response by representatives of Emperor Charles V and his son, Phillip, against members of the Anabaptist wing of the Reformation. This repression prompted the flight of many families to a new homeland in West Prussia.

A full description of these events is beyond the scope of this writing, although additional discussion will follow in Chapter 4. Here we will meet only four individuals who died violently, one because of his militant activism and three because they associated themselves with the Anabaptist movement through adult baptism. Although these four individuals had names that fit within our family trees, we have no evidence they were genetic ancestors. We do claim them as fellow partisans in the Kingdom of God.

Zijbrandt Claesz was a blacksmith from Alkmaar in North Holland. During the tumultuous months when Anabaptists controlled the city of Muenster, declared it the “New Jerusalem” and resisted the combined attempts of Roman Catholic and Lutheran forces to retake the city, Anabaptists in Amsterdam also attempted to mobilize public opinion in support of liberating their city. Jan van Geelen, who had led the take-over earlier that spring of the Olde Klooster monastery in Friesland, was the leader of the Amsterdam activists; Zijbrandt Claesz was a supporter.

During the night of May 10, 1535, he joined a party of 40 men that stormed the Amsterdam courthouse to seize control of that facility. Their efforts briefly succeeded but then failed the next day with fatalities among both the Anabaptists and the courthouse defenders. The eleven surviving Anabaptists (including Zijbrandt) were arrested and summarily executed. No details are available, in part because his name does not appear in Thieleman van Braught’s *Martyrs’ Mirror,* which recounts only the deaths of nonviolent Anabaptists.[8]

Jan Claesz was a bookseller from North Holland. He was (re)baptized by Menno Simons and then collaborated with him by printing and selling 600 copies of Simons’ writings in Holland and Friesland. Claesz also pastored a congregation in Amsterdam. In 1544, he was arrested and put on trial with another Anabaptist. The accusation against him included book publication and the keeping of school and meetings "to introduce errors among the people, which is contrary to the decrees of the Emperor, and our mother the holy church." The court sentenced him to death, "to be executed with the sword, the body to be placed on the wheel, and the head upon a stake."[9]

The account from the *Martyrs' Mirror* goes on:

> "As Claesz went out of the court, he said: 'You citizens bear witness that we die for no other reason than for the true Word of God.' This occurred in the court. Having ascended the scaffold, Claesz audibly addressed the people with these words: 'Hear, ye citizens of Amsterdam; be it known unto you, that I suffer not as a thief or murderer, or because we have sought the property or life of others. However, do not understand me as justifying or exalting myself; but I come with the prodigal son, and depend only on the pure Word of God'."[10]

Willem Jansz resided in Waterland, just north of Amsterdam. A friend and fellow Anabaptist had been condemned to public execution for his faith. When Jansz heard of the sentence, he hurried to the place of the execution to witness the event and perhaps strengthen his friend through the ordeal. When he arrived at the place, the area had already been closed to the public. Jansz persisted in his efforts and by payment of money, convinced the guard to let him enter.

When his friend was brought forward, Jansz called out to him in a loud voice, "Fight valiantly, dear brother!" Immediately Jansz was arrested, thrown into prison, and severely tortured on two separate occasions. He refused to recant and was brought to trial where he was accused of

> "several times (going) to the assembly of the reprobated and accursed sect of Mennonists or Anabaptists; also, about six or seven years ago, rejecting and renouncing the baptism received by him in his infancy of the holy church, (was) rebaptized, and afterwards received the breaking of bread three or four different times, (and) has also exhorted said sect as a teacher."[11]

On March 12, 1569, Jansz was burned alive; he was not first strangled, as was the Dutch custom. His murder is memorialized by a Jan Luyken etching printed in the *Martyrs' Mirror*.

Maeyken Wens, wife of mason Mattheus Wens and mother of several children, was arrested along with other Anabaptist believers in Belgium in October, 1573. She was imprisoned at the Steen castle in Antwerp. From her prison cell, Wens penned five letters, all of which were published in the *Martyrs' Mirror* and one of which is preserved in the Amsterdam Mennonite Archive.

On the morning of October 6, a tongue screw was used to silence Wens. She was taken to the place of execution where a crowd had gathered to witness her death. Adriaen, her 15-year-old son, and Jan Mattheus, her 3-year-old son, voluntarily attended as well. Adriaen fainted when his mother was tied at the stake to be burned. Afterwards, after the crowd had dispersed, he

> "regained consciousness and went to the place where his mother had been burnt, and hunted in the ashes in which he found the screw with which her tongue had been screwed fast, which he kept in remembrance of her."

Adriaen and Jan beside the ashes of their mother are portrayed in a Jan Luyken etching printed in the *Martyrs' Mirror*.[12]

The killing of Anabaptists continued in the Netherlands until 1574 and in Belgium until 1597. At least 800 Anabaptists were martyred in Belgium and perhaps as many as 2,500 in the Netherlands.[13] Given such oppression, it is not hard to understand why many Anabaptists left Flanders, Zealand, Holland and Friesland to start afresh in Prussia.

The blood of the Anabaptists (the Dutch and Flemish martyrs briefly mentioned here as well as French, Swiss, German and Slavic martyrs) changed Europe by demonstrating the primacy of conscience over governments' claims. To be sure, the powers of state and the powers of religion continue until this day to collaborate in mutual self-interest. Nevertheless, the value of separating church and state and creating space within the public realm for the demands of faith is now widely recognized. This is Anabaptism's greatest achievement.

*****

After only sixteen months, Anabaptist rule in Muenster ended with the public display of the dead Anabaptist leaders in iron cages high on St.

Lambert's church tower. Short as it was, the story of the Anabaptist take-over shaped public discourse in Europe long afterward. Mennonite scholars describe Muenster as the most discussed event in Anabaptist history: "No other topic of the Reformation and particularly the Anabaptists has received as much attention throughout the centuries."[14]

Governmental and ecclesiastical leaders focused on the events of Muenster whenever they found it useful to raise fears among the people and rally support for greater repression. What Muenster had demonstrated to the world, these leaders said, was the great threat posed by Anabaptism. It must be suppressed by all means.

Exaggerated though it was, we must acknowledge that 16th century Anabaptists did pose a threat to the status quo. They espoused beliefs and followed practices that were highly attractive to people of that era. These included a reduction in the power of the clergy and a more open exchange of views on the meaning of the Bible, more focus on individual decisions in sealing one's eternal destiny, the practice of religious tolerance, and some loosening of the yoke imposed by princes and bishops. In many parts of Europe, the public was eager to engage these ideas, as evidenced by the spontaneous and tumultuous response to the many itinerant Anabaptist preachers of the time.

After Muenster, Anabaptists no longer regarded violence as an option. Instead, under the leadership of Dirk Philips and Menno Simons, they opposed the use of physical force (including military service) and abandoned broader political activism almost entirely. Yet the official rhetoric about the dangers of Anabaptism continued for 300 years and the specter of Muenster was trotted out whenever the authorities found it convenient to scapegoat the Anabaptists for society's ills.

250 Years in Prussia

What used to be known as Prussia is the area along 200 miles of coastline at the southeast corner of the Baltic Sea. Today, it is part of three nations - Poland, Lithuania and Russia - with Poland controlling the biggest part.

Prussia had three attractive features for Mennonites fleeing persecution in the Low Countries.

One was the active commercial trade already going on between its major cities and the ports of Amsterdam and Antwerp. Travel between the Low Counties and Poland was not difficult.

The second was the Vistula River, which flows north and east out of the Carpathian Mountains, eventually emptying into the Baltic Sea just east of Danzig. During the 16th century, it regularly overflowed and covered the low-lying land in the delta region along the Baltic. After severe flooding in 1540 and 1543, local officials wanted immigrants skilled in the construction of dikes, canals, and wind pumps. The Mennonites from the Low Countries were well suited for such assignments because of their experience in Holland reclaiming land from the North Sea.

The third attractive feature was the relatively tolerant religious environment in Poland. The entire area along the Vistula River was under the rule of the Polish crown. But Danzig, Elbing, Koenigsberg, Culm, Thorn and other Hanseatic League cities enjoyed a significant measure of autonomy. The Roman Catholic Church and the Lutheran Church each had a strong presence. Together, these factors created a patchwork of jurisdictions with distinct and slightly different policies on religious freedom. This created space for religious dissidents like the Mennonites to maneuver and survive.

Beginning in 1530, a few Anabaptists began immigrating to Poland, settling first in the area just outside the Danzig city walls. Others, including Sharon's Klassen ancestors, settled in Elbing, 40 miles to the east at the opposite side of the Delta. These first immigrants practiced the trades, many as weavers.

In 1547, the Danzig city council granted permission for Dutch immigrants to lease the wetlands in the Danzig *Werder,* the area immediately south and east of the city and up to the western bank of the Vistula. At least 10,000 acres were involved. The reclamation efforts proved very successful and the rental income and grain harvests from the land increased sharply. This benefited the City's government and its ruling class, including the Polish king in Warsaw.

Yet the arrangement was almost immediately challenged. In the debates and political infighting that ensued, the continued Mennonite presence in the area was genuinely at risk. But economics carried the day, as articulated by the Danzig city council:

> "To these persons [from the Netherlands] we offered the deserted lands of the low-lying villages of Landau and asked them to restore it at no cost to us. For this, we offered them four years with no payment to us . . . These Netherlanders . . .

> in short time have created wonderful drained land, so that instead of the desolate acres we now have 27 rent-paying farms. The new settlers have increased our annual incomes. . . We have recognized the outstanding industry and skilled planning . . . of these Netherlanders and have taken them into the ranks of regular farmers."[15]

In 1550, the Polish king made an arrangement that enabled Mennonite farmers to settle wetlands along the Tiege River in the central part of the *Gross Werder,* the large area of the Delta between the Vistula and Nogat rivers. The area was expanded through additional leases in 1562 and again in 1578 when the below-sea level area just west of the freshwater Vistula Lagoon was made available for draining and farming. At least 75,000 acres were involved in these leases. This was the largest tract opened to the Mennonite immigrants. Over time it became home to the majority of the Mennonites living in Poland, including my von Riesen, Wiens and Klaassen ancestors.

As noted previously, Mennonites had become part of the vigorous economic activity in Elbing already in the 1530s. Mennonite output was sufficient to pose a competitive threat to the local guilds, which called for their expulsion from the city. In 1550, city officials agreed and evicted the Mennonites.

Enterprising landholders saw this as an opportunity and invited the dispossessed city dwellers to settle the Ellerwald marsh just west of the city and bordering the east bank of the Nogat River. The area consisted of around 9,000 acres of unproductive, desolate land, most of it several feet below sea level. Again the settlers drained the land and put the rich Delta soil to use in productive farming. At some point, Sharon's Wiens ancestors settled there.

During the twenty years after 1565, the lowlands of the *Klein Werder* southwest of Elbing were leased to the Mennonites. This area was just west of Lake Drausen and included perhaps 30,000 acres. At some point, Sharon's Eytzen ancestors settled there.

After the debacle at Muenster, Dutch Anabaptist families also settled around Koenigsberg, at the far eastern end of Vistula Lagoon in modern-day Russia. Nobles of Lutheran persuasion governed this area, called East or Ducal Prussia, and had declared it the first officially Protestant state. Although initially welcoming, the nobles soon changed their minds and expelled the Anabaptists in 1543.

A second attempt began in 1713 when around 100 Dutch Mennonite families secured leases to meadows and lowlands in the Tilset area northeast of Konigsberg. More families joined in 1723. Again, however, the effort came to naught. King Frederick William I expelled the Mennonites in 1724 because the young men, highly coveted by the King for military service because of their tall stature, refused to serve in his army. The King did not evict the Mennonite families involved in the trades, most of whom worked in Koenigsberg; their involvement in the City's commercial life, especially the cloth and lace markets, was too important to disturb.

Nearly all of the wetlands settled by the Dutch Mennonites during this initial period were leased, made available for periods of at least five years and for as many as forty years for drainage, dike construction and maintenance, and the cultivation of grain. Typically, the land was leased to associations, not individuals, and in blocks ranging in size from 250 to 2,500 acres. These leasing associations served both as drainage companies and the core structure of village life.

Over time, however, individual Mennonites and others were able to purchase a substantial portion of the leased lands. By 1787, the 13,600 Mennonites living in the Delta region owned perhaps 400,000 acres, a fact that alarmed their neighbors.[16]

The rural Mennonite settlements on the Delta tended to be culturally homogenous, reflecting the dominant Dutch and Flemish backgrounds of the residents. Although not mentioned here, the Wiebe and Janzen families were well-represented. However, families of other religious persuasions also lived on the Delta, including Lutheran and Catholic families. Somewhere along the line, Germans who had migrated in search of economic opportunity (such as the Rempels) or local Prussians already living in the region (such as the von Riesens) became part of these Mennonite communities, sometimes through marriage and sometimes through conversion and baptism.[17]

*****

In an effort to increase royal revenues, administrators for Poland's king encouraged Mennonites also to settle upriver on underutilized, low-lying ground. Settlements were established throughout the last half of the 16th century, often with members of the Polish nobility acting as the Mennonites' primary advocates and occasional protectors.

Usually these communities were more ethnically and religiously mixed than those on the Delta. A large share of the Mennonite settlers came directly from the Low Countries or from villages and farms on the Delta. But others were refugees from Switzerland, Germany or Moravia, all places where Anabaptism had taken root and its adherents persecuted. In nearly all instances, the Mennonite settlements were on low-lying land close to the Vistula River with Lutheran and Catholic neighbors farming the slightly higher ground nearby. This pattern also contributed more diversity to the experience of the upriver Mennonites.

During the 1540s, the first Dutch Mennonite immigrants settled upriver on the west side of the Vistula near Schwetz. At some point, my Ratzlaff ancestors, of German or Swedish heritage, joined the Mennonite community there.

In 1553, King Sigismund Augustus granted Mennonites the right to lease lands east across the river from Schwetz and just north of Culm. The lease document has been lost and so it is difficult to determine the origin of the first settlers. However, it appears the settlers were primarily immigrants from the Netherlands mixed with a smattering of other Mennonites of Swiss or German background. The Voth family was well-represented there.

In 1568, the first lease was signed with families from the Delta moving upriver. It conveyed lands on the west side of the Vistula near the village of Montau, about five miles south of Neuenburg. According to family historians, around 1597 my Balzer ancestors settled there,[18] perhaps moving from an area further upriver near Culm.

Im 1574, the city council of Thorn entered into a lease with Mennonite farmers and craftsmen. Later, additional Mennonites from the Delta moved south also to farm there. This development marked a reversal of an earlier, aborted attempt by Mennonites to live in this part of Poland. Around 1535, just a few years after Dutch Anabaptists began settling outside the walls of Danzig, a group of 60 Swiss and German Anabaptist families fleeing authorities in Moravia came to the area along the Vistula River. The first Baltzers[19] and Funks in Prussia may have been part of that early migration. Most were banished from the area after only a short time, although a few may have managed to establish permanent homes.

In 1724, the last major Mennonite settlement in Prussia was established a bit below the junction of the Vistula and Nogat rivers and south of the town of Marienburg. Mennonites farmers who had been dispossessed by King Frederick William I from lands in the Tilset area of Ducal Prussia relocated there along the east bank of the river. Delta

Mennonites already owned land there for cattle grazing and they made it available for settlement. My Dueck and Flaming ancestors were part of that settlement.

*****

In 1762, Catherine II, Empress of Russia, issued a declaration inviting German-speaking peoples to immigrate and settle her recently-acquired lands in the Ukraine. Her declaration stated that those responding to her invitation would be guaranteed freedom of speech and religion, could operate their own schools, would be autonomous in matters of local government, and would be exempt from military service. Catherine specifically addressed a supplemental document to the Mennonites in Poland, inviting them to take advantage of her offer, promising them an allotment of land for each family, and indicating that the described rights and privileges would be theirs "for all time."

Apparently the invitation received little attention among Mennonites in Poland until 1786, when it was read aloud at a public meeting in Danzig. The Prussian King Frederick II (also known as Frederick the Great and as "Ole Fritz" to the Mennonites) died in August of that year. While he had been responsible for restrictions in the ability of Mennonites to buy land, he also had been perceived by the Mennonites to be sympathetic to their religious beliefs and financial interests. Mennonites were unnerved by his passing and decided to take another look at the invitation from Catherine II.

The first migration to the Russian lands began in 1787; its members formed the Chortitza Colony along the Dnieper River about 30 miles south of the Russian city of Ekaterinoslav (Dnipropetrovsk). The second and largest migration began in 1803 and continued to the end of the decade; its members formed the Molotschna Colony just 20 miles north of the Sea of Asov and midway between the Russian cities of Melitopol and Berdyansk. Together, these two migrations included around 800 families (5,000 people), about one-third of the Mennonite population in Prussia at the time. Other migrations continued over the next seventy years, some to form other settlements in central Russia. By 1870, at least 10,000 Mennonites had immigrated to Russian lands.

Who went and who stayed and on what basis was that crucial decision made?

All of our ancestors joined the migration; none stayed in Poland. Sharon's great-great-great grandparents, Daniel and Margaretha Eitzen, joined the Chortitza settlement with their six children in 1795. Our other ancestors all moved to Molotschna, some as early as 1803 and others as late as 1836.

We can speculate about their motives. Certainly the increasing demands of the Prussian government and the difficulty in securing more land for faming were the leading reasons. Those who went first – such as the Eitzens – had the fewest resources and the least to lose by relocating. Those who went first also tended to be more conservative and less willing to accommodate the demands of Prussian society.

My Prussian ancestors, Abraham and Margaretha (Wiebe) von Riesen, farmed, traded grain and operated a grist mill in the village of Kalteherberge, just west of the Vistula Lagoon. They probably had more wealth than most. This assumption is basd on the fact that they began life in the Molotschna Colony with four wagons (as compared to the usual one) plus seven horses, fourteen head of cattle, one plow and two harrows. They were part of the 1803 migration, a group whose motives are especially difficult to assess.

Those who migrated later were less eager to leave, either because of their wealth or because of hopes that the Prussian government would ease its demands and accept reasonable accommodations. Three of my ancestral families – the Ratzlaffs, Duecks and Flamings – migrated during the years 1817 - 1821. The Klassens on Sharon's side of the family did not leave Elbing for Russia until the 1830s; similarly, the Balzers and Funks on my side did not leave until 1836.

Historian Peter J. Klassen offers this summary:

> "For those Mennonites who remained in Prussia, the claims of the state and the dominant culture became ever stronger. On the one hand, Mennonites enjoyed a large measure of acceptance, so that the relationship between Lutherans and Mennonites was 'the best that could be imagined.' From another perspective, an observer wrote that Mennonites in Prussia seemed to know 'almost nothing of Menno Simons' except that he rejected infant baptism and the swearing of an oath. In the new Prussia, as in other countries where Mennonites found a home, the quest for a balance between a church's long-held values and beliefs, and the increasingly pervasive demands of the state presented challenges that could not be ignored. For many, a 'godly' state had made obedience

> appropriate and right; for others, emigration seemed the correct response if their traditional faith was to be maintained."[20]

Klassen notes that in 1915, as the German nation mobilized for what later became known as World War I, the pastor of the Danzig Mennonite Church, H G. Mannhardt, was given the honor of speaking on behalf of the City's clergy to a large public gathering. His speech described the purpose of the German nation as a "struggle for liberty" against the unjust hostility of enemies who were filled with "envy and hatred" and "destructive rage" against a righteous Germany. He expressed gratitude to God for the German nation and called on his audience to be ready to fight and die for the fatherland.

Not all Mennonites agreed, and the history of the Mennonites living along the Vistula during the late 19th and early 20th centuries is replete with stories of different congregations taking somewhat different positions. But by World War II, the teaching in German Mennonite congregations against taking up arms had lost its vitality. Most Mennonites saw no contradiction between the demands of Caesar and the demands of God and very few pursued a path other than that required by the Nazi regime.

Russian Interlude

The Mennonites were not the only people who responded to the invitation of Catherine II; Lutheran families from Germany began accepting the Czarina's invitation in 1763 and other Protestant groups and Catholics from eastern Europe emigrated too. In fact, the 10,000 Mennonites who migrated constituted only about 10 percent of the German-speaking peoples who settled in Russia during the 19th century.[21] By and large, the Russian policy during this time attempted to attract experienced, capable people who would become well-established, fill lightly populated areas, and strengthen Russia's ability to compete economically with European powers. Areas in both south and central Russia were opened for settlement.

As part of its immigration policy, the Russian government allocated newly-opened lands in a way that kept the immigrant groups separated from one another. By maintaining distance, the government hoped to minimize religious strife and the need to provide public services. By and large, the immigrant groups (including the Mennonites) were pleased with this arrangement as it ensured their neighbors would be like-minded in matters of religious and culture.

The land in south Russia was a level plain with few trees. The top soil was rich and 18 inches thick. It wasn't as well-suited for dairying and the raising of livestock as the lands along the Vistula River but was ideal for growing grain, an activity Mennonite farmers already knew a good bit about.

According to historian James Urry,

> "All land was placed in the perpetual and incontestable possession of the colony as a corporate group, and could not be sold or mortgaged to outsiders. Each Mennonite colonist received a separate allotment of 160 acres, which they and their descendants could use in perpetuity. This allotment could not be subdivided, but, while the 1764 law specified that only the youngest son could inherit the property, Mennonites, through provisions granted in their 1800 *Privilegium*, could follow their own inheritance customs. Usually the eldest Mennonite son inherited the land and homestead, but he had to compensate his siblings for their portion of the estate."[22]

The colonists lived in compact villages, but the land was assigned to individual farmers, often in long, narrow strips. Pasturelands were consolidated and shared. Because of the corporate ownership of the land, there was a significant degree of land use regulation via common agreement.

The resettlement experience was difficult; it required the settlers to start from scratch, constructing houses and barns and breaking the sod. In general, however, Mennonites were delighted with the opportunity to establish their own communities apart from neighbors who had different religious beliefs and far from meddlesome governments. After many years of confrontation and uncertainty in Poland, it was a huge relief to be by themselves. Mennonite prospects for success seemed bright.

However, the isolation of the Ukraine created its own problems. Many Mennonites never learned the Russian language and relatively few made strong connections with Russian society or non-Mennonite neighbors. In Poland, many Mennonites had lived as a local minority in a mixed society and had acquired the language and negotiating skills appropriate to such a context. In Russia the Mennonites remained separate and apart, "outsiders" long after settling there.

As historian John N. Klassen notes, self-government was a mixed blessing.

> "For the first time in their history, these Mennonites were not immediately subject to the government of their country; the civil administrators of their colonies were drawn from their own ranks. They had had no experience of this kind and also no civil leaders. There was no separation of civil and church powers. If there were differences of opinion between church and civil leaders, it was usually the church council that ruled, and thus was supported by the civil arm.
>
> "Thus the Russian Mennonites constituted a kind of 'state within a state.' In doing so they relinquished a number of insights of the Early Church and of the first Anabaptists. Instead of just electing preachers and elders, they now also elected alderman and mayors, teachers and school boards, and even police officers. In the beginning it seemed very strange to the individual that one 'brother' would be placed above another 'brother'."[23]

*****

The Molotschna Colony, home to all of Sharon's and my ancestors for at least a portion of the 19th century, consisted in 1865 of 60 villages and 25,000 inhabitants.[24] The villages lay alongside the rivers and streams flowing through Colony lands, thus providing easy access to water for livestock. Typically, the distance between villages was only a mile or two.

A village of 450 residents included perhaps twenty families working a "full farm" of 165-175 acres, ten families working a "half-farm," and another thirty families that either rented their homes or owned a small acreage for gardening and a few head of livestock. The adult males in these non-farming households worked as farm laborers for wages or as self-employed tradesmen. Together with low-lying areas and pastureland, such a village was responsible for 5,000 acres of land.

At the beginning, all of the Colony's residents related to one congregation under the authority of an elder. Over time, a degree of diversity emerged due to new congregations under the authority of their own elders. By 1865 ten congregations had been organized, offering residents some variety in worship styles, leadership and theology. All but two of the congregations continued to function as branches of the original root, known as the *Gross Gemeinde* (Big Church). Two groups – the *Kleine Gemeinde* (Little Church) and the Mennonite Brethren – severed their ties with the established network; their congregations functioned separately. Each of these three religious groups became an important factor in our families' stories during the 19th Century.

The *Kleine Gemeinde* reflected a preference for looking to history for guidance in life. The Bible, the writings of Menno Simons and the early Anabaptists, and the *Martyrs' Mirror* were much more authoritative for them than contemporary experience. They practiced strict church discipline. They wanted an embodied faith that showed itself in the habits and routines of living; thus, they emphasized social separatism to enable members to maintain those valued habits and routines. While recognizing that others also could be Christian, the *Kleine Gemeinde* assumed the many worldly influences of life on "the broad road" would usually extinguish the desire to live in the way taught by Jesus in the Gospels.

The Mennonite Brethren, which did not figure significantly in our family history until the Minnesota chapter, reflected a more open stance toward the world. Although not commonly considered progressive in our current milieu, during the latter half of the 19th century the Mennonite Brethren filled that spot within the Russian Mennonite world. They valued education, ecumenical relationships with other Christians, mission activity among unbelievers, new church practices to more fully engage adults and youth, and social and business contacts with people outside traditional ethnic boundaries. They emphasized a heartfelt faith, authenticated through an emotional conversion experience at a specific time and place. Being Mennonite was not that important to this group; what was important was being Christian.

All of Sharon's ancestors and the entire maternal side of my family were part of the largest of the three groups, the *Gross Gemeinde.* As the Mennonite religious establishment, it was the body against which the others defined themselves. Because it was more varied than the other two groups, it is more difficult to characterize. Some of its congregations nurtured a vital and life-changing faith while others were hidebound, requiring only pious conformity. Few, however, emphasized the teachings of Menno Simons or the early Anabaptists and many were content simply to maintain the traditions of the previous generation. In Russia, at least parts of the *Gross Gemeinde* became similar to what the early Anabaptists had rebelled against: a church that shared power with civil authorities in support of the status quo.

Where in Molotschna Colony did our ancestors live? For many, we can name the specific villages and a few of those place-names are noted in the Appendix.

Unfortunately, we don't have journals or accounts that tell us specific information about their lives. Instead, we are left to piece together impressions based on occasional school attendance registers, census reports, and church records. In this fashion, we can assemble information about when a family moved from one village to another, what work it relied on to make a living, and the theological emphases it likely encountered in congregational worship. Such information, while helpful, falls far short of what we want to know about their lives.

Due to the prominence of my von Riesen/Friesen ancestors in the *Kleine Gemeinde* and the interest historians have shown in that small religious group, we have more information about them. The most notable member was my great-great-great-great-grandfather, Abraham von Riesen. He was 22 when he accompanied his father and mother from Poland to the Molotschna Colony. Soon after he began using Friesen as his last name; it was a common surname among his neighbors and its use avoided the false connotations of nobility that some in Russia associated with the name von Riesen.

Abraham married Katharina Wiebe at age 25 and a year later, in the 1808 census, was listed as owning a full farm adjacent to that of his parents in Ohrloff. Other property included one horse, two head of cattle, 47 sheep, thirteen loads of hay and a quantity of unthreshed grain.

In 1817, Abraham was elected deacon of the Ohrloff congregation, the founding religious body of the *Gross Gemeinde* in the Colony. Just a year later, he left that network of congregations and became a member of the *Kleine Gemeinde.* He was elected as a minister in that group in 1823 and subsequently became responsible for its official correspondence. Many of his letters and sermons and some of his poetry survive. Two excerpts are included in Chapter 5.

Abraham was elected as leading elder of the *Kleine Gemeinde* in 1838 and served for nine years. In that capacity, he often represented his congregation in discussions with other Colony leaders on matters involving conflict or controversy. Around 600 adults and children were part of his congregations when he stepped down in 1847.[25]

Along with a brother back in Danzig, Peter von Riesen, Abraham translated, published, and distributed writings of Dutch Mennonite church leaders, thereby making those available to the Russian colonists, most of whom no longer read or spoke Dutch. Their first project occurred in 1827 when they published *Mirror of Greed*, a 17th century text written in Dutch by Pieter Pieters. According to Delbert Plett, "It was the first book published" in Russia by a Mennonite. Later, Abraham and his brother translated and published the works of Menno Simons and made those available to people in the Mennonite colonies.[26]

Abraham died in 1849, just days short of his 67th birthday.

His son, Jacob W. Friesen, also was a well-known figure in the Molotschna Colony. He lived in Blumstein, just east of Ohrloff, and served as mayor there during the 1840s. He was elected a deacon by the *Kleine Gemeinde* in 1850.

*****

Farming was the preferred way to earn a living in the Russian colonies as it led to economic independence and sometimes wealth. But under the terms of the founding documents, the land could not be divided among children; only one child could inherit. Furthermore, excess colony lands were not available for purchase. Thus, by 1860, about two-thirds of the working age adults were landless.

This economic disparity had profound political implications because only landowners had the opportunity to vote on village decisions. Consequently, those elected to administrative positions nearly always represented the interests of the well-to-do. This even spilled over into church life, where the elders and ministers also tended to be members of the dominant socioeconomic group.

This was a particular concern for the tradition-oriented *Kleine Gemeinde,* who were convinced that farming was essential to maintaining the separated, ascetic life to which they felt called. Generally, their congregations followed a practice of providing interest-free loans to younger members who wanted to buy land. This effectively enabled about two-thirds of its members to acquire farmland. But the farms were geographically dispersed, making it difficult to gather for fellowship and worship.

As disparities in wealth among Colony residents widened, the landless began to more aggressively agitate for land reform. Some of this is described more fully in Chapter 4. The leaders of the *Kleine Gemeinde* also felt this pressure, despite the fact that a larger share of their members owned land. In the future, the problem would only get worse.

In 1861, the Russian government freed the serfs, enabling them to leave the estates of Russian nobles and pursue their own fortunes. With serfs no longer a reliable source of labor, estate owners began selling land. This opened an opportunity for the Mennonites to acquire land at a reasonable cost and establish "daughter colonies" in the immediate area.

Starting in 1863 and throughout the remainder of that decade, the *Kleine Gemeinde* bought or leased large tracts for the purpose of establishing colonies for its members. Its largest (18,000 acres) and most successful venture was Borozenko; it was located 75 miles northwest of Molotschna and 30 miles straight west of the Chortitza Colony. Six villages were established in the new colony. During the years 1865-67, around 120 families (about 800 people) settled there.[27]

All of my Friesen and Ratzlaff ancestors joined this resettlement effort, including Gerhard Friesen, my great-grandfather, who lived at Borozenko with his uncle and aunt, Abraham and Anna Friesen. It required them to again start from scratch with the construction of homes and barns and the plowing of the unbroken grassland.

As described by *Kleine Gemeinde* advocate Delbert Plett, the story of the Borozenko Colony is noteworthy for several reasons. It included many men who sold established farms in order to be part of the new venture. It was financed entirely by private funds, without subsidies from the established colonies or from the Russian government. It was open only to *Kleine Gemeinde* members. This paints a picture of a self-confident group that was willing to sacrifice for the well-being of its less prosperous members.[28] It also suggests the group was becoming ever more separatist in its attempt to live ethically. Not only did they seek to live apart from Russian residents and German colonists of other persuasions, but also from less traditional Mennonites.

In short order, the new colony proved its economic viability. Yet by 1874, nearly all of the farms there were up for sale as the Colony's residents prepared to move yet again, this time to North America.

*****

In late 1870, rumors circulated through the Mennonite colonies concerning a Russian government plan to follow European governments in requiring military service of all young Russian men. As rumored, this new law would not recognize the historic exemption for the sons and grandsons of immigrants who had relocated in reliance on the promises of Czarina Catherine II.

This government plan seemed to be part of a broader effort to unify the Russian people culturally and economically and prepare them to stand together in support of "mother Russia" in an age of nationalism. Other aspects of the grand plan included greater Russian government oversight of curriculum and teacher training in private schools and greater emphasis on Russian language instruction in the schools. For some Mennonites, this was as alarming as the possibility of military conscription.

Acting quickly, the colonists assembled a delegation to St. Petersburg to seek clarification of how this proposed law would affect their young men. In February, 1871 the delegates met with the Minister of War. The meeting did not go well. The Minister was surprised that the entire meeting was conducted in the German language and that no Mennonite delegate spoke Russian. "You have been in Russia for seventy years and still cannot speak our language? That is a sin!" he is reported to have said.

Throughout 1871, the picture gradually became clearer. The Russian government seemed prepared to consider service alternatives that did not involve the carrying of weapons, but it was not willing to grant a blanket exemption from national service.

This ignited debate among the Mennonite colonists. Some were prepared to accept an arrangement whereby young men served in the medical corps or the forestry service; this was the position of the more "progressive" Mennonites, including the leading congregations in the Molotschna Colony and most of the Mennonite Brethren. Others said such a compromise would be contrary to the teachings of their faith; the Margenau-Alexanderwohl and Pordenau congregations took this position as well as by the *Kleine Gemeinde* and the generally more conservative Chortitza congregations.

In the fall of 1872, the more conservative groups sent their own delegates, including Abraham L. Friesen, first to St. Petersburg and then to Yalta to convey opposition to national conscription. Although they were well-received and had a meeting with Governor General Kotzebu in Yalta, the delegates returned home convinced national service was inevitable. For them, this left no choice but emigration from Russia to some other land.

Early in 1873, the colonists sent twelve delegates to North America to inspect available lands and seek guarantees regarding the operation of their own schools and an exemption from military service. These delegations returned by late summer with their reports.

The Canadian government offered large, compact tracts of free land in Manitoba where the Mennonites could replicate their village life in Russia. It also promised a complete exemption from military service and the right to conduct separate schools. United States President Ulysses Grant met with members of the delegation, but told them only Congress could give them what they wanted. In 1874, Congress debated a bill that would have enabled the Mennonites to secure up to 500,000 contiguous acres for a colony. But the bill met stiff opposition and never came up for a vote.

To those who had decided to emigrate, the advantages of each location were clear. The United States had the milder climate and better access to urban markets for the sale of agricultural products. Canada offered stronger protections for their religious and cultural values and the opportunity to continue living in closed communities. The choice was difficult, dividing some families.

Apart from destination, those emigrating had the arduous task of disposing of their property. With around one-third of the Mennonite population leaving, prices plummeted and few sellers received full value for what they sold. This was especially true in places such as Borozenko Colony where nearly everyone left at the same time.

In the end, around 18,000 Mennonites emigrated from South Russia during these years with 10,500 choosing the United States and 7,500 Canada. According to historians Cornelius Krahn and Adolf Ens, most who settled in the United States tended to be from the Molotschna Colony where they had "already adjusted themselves to the economic and cultural life . . . to a larger degree than the more conservative groups." For those who settled in Canada, what was most important were guarantees "that would safeguard the future of their traditional economic, cultural, and religious life."[29]

Most of Sharon's and my ancestors fit that general pattern. That is, most had lived in the Molotschna Colony and they settled in Minnesota. The Friesens were an exception; although members of the *Kleine Gemeinde,* they did not settle in Manitoba, but chose Nebraska instead. In large part, this was due to the influence of Cornelius Jansen, a highly regarded Prussian Mennonite businessman and former resident of

Berdyansk in south Russia. Jansen was married to Helena von Riesen, a cousin of many of the Friesens. Jansen actively promoted Nebraska, and he and his family settled there himself at the same time as the new immigrants.[30]

*****

Within nearly 500 years of family history, the time in Russia was comparatively short. For great-great grandmother Anna Funk Wiens, it was only 39 years from the time she left Poland until she reached Philadelphia harbor and made her way west to her new home in Minnesota. Similarly, Gerhard Klassen and his wife, Maria Reimer, Heinrich Balzer, and David Flaming (great-great-grandparents all) spent their youth in Poland, married and raised their families in Molotschna Colony, and then emigrated again in their fifties.

Other ancestral families were in Russia a few years longer. But even for the Eytzens, who arrived in Russia first, the entire experience ended after only 80 years.

Looking back at the Russian interlude from our perspective, it was a time of sacrifice and deprivation during the initial years followed by prosperity and peace. With rare exceptions, no armies occupied their villages or requisitioned their grain or livestock. Most achieved a measure of economic self-sufficiency. Government interference was minimal. Few experienced persecution.

Yet by the middle years of the 1870s, our ancestors felt compelled to leave Russia and start over yet again in the American Midwest. I find this surprising. Their ancestors had lived for 250 years amid the push-and-pull of Prussia and had managed to remain true to their faith. Surely those who lived in Russia in the 1870s had opportunities to reach similar accommodations with the evolving Russian policies on education and conscription. Were they too impatient with the thought of negotiating with the Russians, too sensitive about the stretching of their scruples, too doubtful of God working through the politics of give-and-take?

With the benefit of hindsight, their decisions to leave can be praised as far-sighted. Within 45 years of their departure, during the chaos at the end of World War I, terrible violence visited the Mennonite colonies. During the 1920s and 1930s, as the Bolshevik Revolution was implemented in their communities, many died of starvation or were exiled to certain death in Siberia. The persecution by the Soviet government was so severe that a Mennonite presence in the Ukraine ended entirely. Our ancestors escaped all of this by leaving early.

Starting Over in the U.S.A.

Sharon's Klassen ancestors settled just a few miles south of Mountain Lake, as did her paternal Wiebe ancestors. Her maternal ancestors chose land in Carson Township, six-to-eight miles west and north of Mountain Lake. My maternal ancestors did the same. In contrast, my paternal ancestors put down roots in Nebraska.

Sharon's Paternal Klassen Line

As recounted at the beginning of this chapter, through the descendants of Abraham G. Klassen, the immigrant who died at age 28, the Klassen family has been continuously present in the Mountain Lake community since 1875.

The descendents of a younger brother, Peter, added considerably to the Klassen presence in the community. Peter's nine children all married, most had large families, and most stayed in the Mountain Lake area. As a result, Sharon attended school with many third cousins with whom she shared her great-great-grandparents, Gerhard and Maria Klassen. Interesting as this may be now, it was seldom thought worthy of mention as Sharon was growing up.

The widow of Gerhard, the older brother who also died young, moved to Henderson, Nebraska in 1879. She remarried and had a second family there. Her eldest son, also named Gerhard Klassen, died in the Philippines at age 31. He was a soldier, serving in the U.S. campaign to suppress the independence movement of the Filipino people.

Maria was the older Klassen daughter. She already had four children when she immigrated in 1875 with her husband, Johann Friesen. During the late 1870s, they also relocated to Henderson, Nebraska.

The younger Klassen daughter, Anna, lived with her husband, Peter Schultz, and their ten children in the Mountain Lake area until early 1902, when they joined 157 other families from Mountain Lake in relocating to central Saskatchewan.[31] Peter helped organize and lead the migration and later became prominent across the prairie provinces as a pastor and churchman.[32] The elderly Gerhard and Maria followed their children to Canada; she died in Langham in 1905 and he in 1910.

Thus, of the second generation Klassens who settled in Minnesota, only daughter-in-law Elizabeth and son Peter remained. Both had big families and left many third generation Klassens who lived in the area.

Sharon's Paternal Wiebe Line

William Wiebe, his first wife, Sara Dickman, and their three children began their journey west from Marianthal, at the far southeast corner of Molotschna. From there they traveled by train across Europe to Antwerp and then crossed the Atlantic on the S.S. State of Nevada, reaching New York City harbor in August, 1875. William was 32 years of age at the time. We have no information about his family of origin.

After arriving in Minnesota, the Wiebe family filed a homestead claim to the northern 80 acres in the northeast quarter of Section 22 of Mountain Lake Township, the same section in which Abraham Klassen had claimed a homestead a few weeks earlier. Fifteen years later, in September 1890, the Wiebes purchased from Elias Drake 80 acres immediately to the north, along the eastern edge of the southeast quarter of Section 15. The price per acre ($7.50) suggests it was bare land without any improvements.

William and Sara had two more children in Minnesota, the last in mid-May, 1879. Sara died a month later, perhaps from complications related to childbirth. Although we can not be certain, it is likely the midwife for the delivery was Elizabeth Voth Klassen.

With five children under the age of ten years and the work of a new homestead all around him, we can imagine William in desperate need of help. Had extended family members lived nearby, they may have filled the gap. That option was not available and so William swiftly pursued marriage. He and Justina Wiens Koehn married on July 27, 1879.

As a young woman, Justina Wiens married Johann Koehn and lived with him in the village of Alexanderwohl, at the center of Molotschna Colony. After the Russian government signaled its intention to change the conscription law, Alexanderwohl's residents were among the first to emigrate and the only village group to do so as a unit. They arrived in New York City on September 3, 1874 and then made their way to Kansas where they settled on lands in Marion and McPherson counties. Justina and Johann had two children in Russia and one more in 1875 after their arrival in Kansas. Sometime later, Johann died.

This leaves many questions unanswered, including the circumstances around Justina's widowhood and how a Kansas widow and a Minnesota widower managed to find each other and marry so quickly after the death of William's first wife. The communications must have occurred entirely by mail. We can imagine someone served as matchmaker, alerting these two of their mutual need. The most likely possibility is Justina's sister, Maria Wiens Hiebert, who lived on a farm a few miles west of Mountain Lake. The Hieberts had crossed the Atlantic on the same ship as the Wiebe family; perhaps Maria Hiebert became acquainted with William then.

Justina and William's first child, a son, was born in 1880 and their first daughter in October 1881. In all, they had eight children together in addition to the five children William brought into the marriage and the three Justina brought into the marriage. It made for a complicated family structure. Growing up, Sharon recalls her father saying that his mother's family was "too complicated to explain."

We can't be certain, but there are indications the family related to the *Bruderthaler* congregation (Evangelical Mennonite Brethren) and joined the migration to Saskatchewan organized by that group in the spring of 1899. The first bit of evidence is the timing of the Wiebes' land sale in June of that same year. Second is the fact that in Cottonwood County files, there is no record of any kind related to William or Justina after their land sale. The third clue is the marriages of two of their sons in Saskatchewan and Alberta around 1910. Children from one of those marriages later lived in British Columbia and remained in contact with their first cousins back in Mountain Lake.

What we are certain of is that the Wiebes' oldest daughter, Justina, stayed in Mountain Lake. She was the lovely 17-year-old who married Abraham Klassen in early 1889 and moved into a new house he built for her in Mountain Lake Their son, William, became Sharon's father.

Sharon's Maternal Eytzen Line

Johann Eytzen, a recent widower with four children, arrived in New York City in November 1875 He probably reached Minnesota around Christmas, just as winter temperatures were dropping below zero. We don't know how he spent that first year. Perhaps he worked as a laborer for another farmer. Certainly he grieved for his wife, who had died only days before the family left Russia. His 21-year-old daughter, Katharina, carried responsibility for the home. Fifteen-year-old Jacob was expected to work like a man.

In early 1877, Johann purchased an 80-acre farm in the south half of the southwest quarter of Section 13 in Carson Township from Dietrich and Catherine Walde. The Waldes had occupied the premises for two years and had made improvements during that time. We can assume this from the price ($1,345), which was higher than the going rate for virgin land. Most likely, buildings had been constructed, trees planted, and some of the land had been plowed and put into crops.

We know very little about the Eytzens during their first decades in Minnesota. Their farm was just two miles east of the local Mennonite Brethren meetinghouse, built in 1885. I expect they found that convenient and a source of support.

It was at that church where son Jacob, as a 32-year-old man, noticed Maria Wiebe, the daughter of a local farmer. Jacob approached one of the ministers and told him of his interest in marrying Maria. The minister conveyed this information to Maria, who agreed to the proposal. There was no courtship. They married on May 26, 1893.

We assume they lived with Jacob's father, Johann, on his farm. Children soon arrived: Marie in 1894, John in 1895, Katharina in 1896, Sara and Jacob in 1898, Suzanne in 1900. That was just the start; there were thirteen births in all, the last of whom was Sharon's mother, Esther.

Apparently Jacob and his father enjoyed some financial success. In September 1901, Jacob purchased 160 acres in Section 31 from his brother-in law, Abraham J. Wiebe, for $4,480. Wiebe had purchased the land earlier in the year, most of it from a railroad company, and had paid $2,457 or about fifteen dollars an acre. We can assume the difference in price reflected improvements the two men made to the property over the course of that year, including a house for Jacob and Maria's growing family. A year later, father Johann sold his 80 acre farm in Section 13 and moved in with his son and daughter-in-law.

That farm was known as "the Eytzen place" throughout the 20th century. The house was enlarged in 1915 and made spacious enough for thirteen children plus a grandpa. A larger barn was added at about the same time; it was used for milking. Jacob supplemented their income by leasing portions of the farm for gravel removal. The children attended grades one-to-eight at the school building along the south edge of Section 29, about a mile and one-half northeast of their home.

Esther carried mixed memories of her childhood. Her father was 54 when she was born. By nature a sober and strict man, his advancing years left him with little warmth and flexibility for his family. Esther's siblings sometimes made matters worse by teasing their youngest sister about being the thirteenth child. Esther was left with nagging doubts about whether she was welcome in her own family. It was a wound she carried her entire life. Writing in 1977, she said:

"Because I was teased a lot at home and by others, often publicly, I became afraid to talk for fear something I'd say would again be used to tease me. To this day I find it very difficult to express my inner feelings."

Yet she had many warm childhood memories, particularly of her mother and of adventures with her sisters. Here is just one.

"One summer when it was haying time, Justina and I went along to stamp the [loose] hay in order to get more hay on each load. It was a big load and made bigger since there was so little left [in the field] that no one wanted to make another trip. Again and again, we heard, 'Girls, it's a big load. Stamp it good! It's going to be a dandy to tip.' We loaded it and started out sitting like queens way on top, the pitch forks securely placed, but rather close. From the start, I shook with fear that we would tip, partly because of the way my brothers talked and partly because we had a ridge to cross which always gave me the creeps. Wouldn't you know that while crossing this ridge it happened – we tipped. Justina and I were buried under the hay. . . . Luckily we were unharmed. I remember screaming to let the boys know we were alive."

Of Jacob and Maria's ten children who lived to adulthood, six went on to live in the Mountain Lake area. Three lived most of their years on the west coast, and one in Wisconsin.

When Sharon was in her early teens, she cooked and cleaned for Nettie and Edwin Eytzen, a grandson of Jacob. The farm passed out of the Eytzen family during the debt crisis of the mid-1980s. In the spring of 2008, the trees were taken out and the buildings leveled and burned. The land where the farmyard once stood is now tilled and planted with no remaining evidence of the vibrant activity that once transpired there.

Sharon's Maternal Wiebe Line

Johann Wiebe was born in the village of Gnadenfeld in Molotschna Colony. We have no information about his parents and thus do not know if he was distantly related to the William Wiebe described above. Johann married Justina Rempel in 1868 and had five children with her during their seven years of marriage. Three of those children lived to adulthood, including Sharon's grandmother, Maria. Justina died in 1875; her passing may have interrupted Johann's plan to join other Mennonite families immigrating to the United States.

Two years later he married Maria Balzer, a twice-widowed 31-year-old woman who had two children from two previous marriages. She was the oldest daughter of Heinrich and Katharina Balzer. Together, Johann and Maria had five children, four of them born in Russia.

After departing from Bremen, Germany, the family arrived in New York City in June 1886 and settled in Carson Township by homesteading the northeast quarter of Section 32, just one-half mile south of where her parents already lived. There they built their home and other structures. A year later, the Wiebes purchased the southeast quarter of Section 32 for $1,400. The purchase included a body of water known as Maiden Lake; the price suggests the land was unimproved.

We know they attended the Mennonite Brethren church located in Section 15 of the Township because that is where their daughter, Maria, met her husband, Jacob Eytzen, who she married without courtship. Maria's sister, Sarah, married Peter Balzer, youngest son of Heinrich and Katharina. Their brother, Abraham J. Wiebe, married Susie Ewert and lived on a second building site on the Wiebe land, just south of the original homestead. The families formed by those three marriages lived two-to-three miles of one another. Sharon's mother had life-long friendships with the cousins from those families who remained in the area, especially Emma Wiebe Friesen and her brother, Menno Wiebe.

In addition to farming, Abraham J. Wiebe served the Carson Mennonite Brethren Church as its lead minister from 1916 until 1939. He passed the farm to his son, Jacob A. Wiebe, who worked it until the late 1960s when it was purchased by the Espenson family.

Sharon and I have many memories of Maiden Lake there on the Wiebe land. In August 1961, when Sharon was twelve, Rev. Loyal Martin baptized her there into the Carson Mennonite Brethren Church. On hot summer evenings, families from the community gathered there to swim. During cold winter nights, our church youth group built huge bonfires on the ice and hosted skating parties. When Sharon was in ninth grade, we shared our first kiss at such an event.

Three of the children in Johann's second family (with Maria Balzer Wiebe) lived to adulthood and married. One was a pastor, the second a pastor's wife, and the third a missionary to India. The children of those marriages (Hiebert, Ewert, Wiebe) made up a "Who's Who" of the broader Mennonite Brethren community in the United States as they provided leadership in church institutions during much of the 20th century. Some of their names appear in footnote 6 to this chapter.

After Maria's death in 1922, Johann moved to a new brick house in town next to the Mennonite Brethren church. He died in 1929 at age 85.

Berry's Maternal Wiens Line

Jacob and Anna Funk Wiens, together with six of their eight children, arrived in Philadelphia in July 1875 on the same ship as the Sharon's Klassen ancestors. We can imagine them traveling in one another's company all the way to the railroad depot in Mountain Lake. Anna probably kept her eye on her grandmother's trunk, the one made nearly a hundred years earlier in Poland and now on display at the Heritage House Museum in Mountain Lake.

A few days later, on August 16th, Jacob appeared in the federal land office in New Ulm and filed a homestead claim to an 80-acre tract in the northwest quarter of Section 28 in Carson Township. His sons, Johann and Peter, also filed homestead claims: Peter to the other half of the northwest quarter of Section 28 and Johann to 80 acres in the southeast quarter of Section 18.

Nearly six years later, they "proved up their claims" by filing affidavits with the land office. Jacob's stated he had been erected a 26 feet by 26 feet frame house (one and one-half story) on the property and occupied it in September 1875. Also, he stated he had constructed a 28 feet by 40 feet stable, dug a well, planted one acre of trees, and put thirty acres into crops. He valued these improvements at $700. The affidavit was accepted and the U.S. government conveyed him title to the land.

Near the time of father Jacob's death in 1891, his homestead was sold to the youngest son, Heinrich. It remains in the Wiens family; currently it is owned and occupied by Harry Wiens, Heinrich's grandson.

Two of the three Wiens daughters moved with their husbands to Oklahoma and South Dakota. But the other daughter and the five sons stayed put and the Wienses became a strong agricultural presence in Carson Township during the first decade of the 20th century. In the aggregate, the six children resident in the township owned nearly 1,600 acres. Over the years, Johann expanded his holdings to 353 acres and built a second farm site toward the center of Section 18. Johann's oldest son, John, (my grandfather) took over the farming operation after his marriage in 1911.

My mother had pleasant memories of her childhood there. She attended school in Delft, made two life-long friends in first grade, and learned to speak English. In 1982, she wrote this about life on the farm:

> "Growing up with seven brothers and sisters was a good experience. We had good times, made our own games since we didn't have many toys. We also fought and argued. There never was enough money, it seemed, and mother sewed and patched and skimped so they could pay the bills and feed and clothe all of us.
>
> "We all had to help and yet after I learned to read, I would sneak away to read a book I so wanted to finish, instead of the work mother had for me.
>
> "Mother would bake big loaves of home made bread, and rhubarb pie in a big cake pan. And take buttered slices of bread and the pie to the field where father and the boys were stacking hay. And we'd all sit in the shade of a big tree and eat that good lunch."

Berry's Maternal Balzer Line

Heinrich and Katharina (Reimer) Balzer arrived in New York City harbor in early July, 1878. With them were their four youngest children, all teenagers: Katharina, Jacob, Susanna, and Peter. Writing in 1951, their granddaughter Elizabeth (Lizzie) recalled this family story:

> "The trip in those days took very long. They were on the ship [from Bremen, Germany] a few weeks but they had their own food: cured meat, hams, dark bread, toasted zwieback and others eats, in real big chests."

They traveled directly to Mountain. Lake, where I imagine someone from the Wiens family met them. In Russia, the two families had been part of the same congregation, Margenau-Alexanderwohl, so they likely were well acquainted.

Son Henry Balzer and his wife Sarah Klaassen probably also met them at the station; they had come to Minnesota two years earlier and had been living with Sarah's parents on a farm in Dale Township.

Later that same month, Heinrich Sr. purchased 120 acres of land in Section 29 of Carson Township from the Sioux City and St. Paul

Railroad. The price was S840. The land lay immediately west of the Jacob Wiens Sr. homestead, indicating the close relationship between the two families. It lay immediately north of the land purchased by Aron Reimer, a brother to Katharina.

The first order of business was to build shelters from the weather. Again, Aunt Lizzie provided details:

> "They had to build their homes almost out of nothing. They would make bricks with earth and mix something in it. They would build sod houses which were very warm, of course house and barn in one. The roof was made of long grass which did grow in many places in those years. They were fortunate to get some windows already, so their home was real nice. The walls were white washed and the floor was sand. They had a stove built within the house with which they warmed themselves.
>
> "They plowed their land with oxen and whenever the oxen were thirsty and they would see water, they would just run and drink. When they would go places they just drove on big lumber wagons which surely were made by themselves. Later on they had horses and all the work was done with horses.
>
> "They dug their wells by hand and pulled the water up with pails. If they were progressive, they would have a framework over the well where the rope was attached and a pail on each end of the rope.
>
> "In those years my mother never had a washing machine. She did all her family laundry in a wooden tub, which gave many backaches. The stove mother did her baking in was made of bricks and it was heated with hay. I have been told it was the nicest bread!"

Within the first year, the sod house and barn were replaced by more permanent structures. We know few details. During the time I lived on the farm some eighty years later, the only evidence I saw of those first buildings was a small barn, perhaps 14 feet by 24 feet with a peaked roof, an attic area above the ground level, and a lean-to affixed to the back. We used it as a cattle shed. Besides its old and decrepit appearance, it was distinguished by plaster-and-lathe walls and ceiling, which indicated it had once been used as a residence. We never spoke of it as the home of the first Balzer settlers, but in retrospect I recognize it was.

Daughter Katharine died in 1880 at age 21. Daughter Susanna married Abram Ewert in 1884; they bought land in the northwest quarter of that same Section 29. Back in Russia, eldest daughter Maria married Johann Wiebe in 1877; they settled in Carson Township in 1886.

After son Jacob's marriage to Maria Klaassen (Sarah Klaassen's sister) on the day after Christmas in 1883, he and older brother Henry each bought land in Section 19 from the railroad. Jacob paid $560 for 80 acres. The land was unimproved, so Jacob and Maria began by building shelters for themselves and their animals. Both parcels overlooked Rat Lake to the east.

In 1899, Jacob and Marie purchased 183 acres in the north half of Section 20, overlooking Rat Lake to the southwest. My grandmother, Sarah, lived there during her teenage years and until her marriage in 1911 to John Wiens, who lived less than a mile away. Marie died of cancer in 1907; Jacob remarried two years later.

Youngest son Peter married a neighbor girl, Sarah Wiebe, in 1888. After living with parents for a time, they bought the Balzer farm (consisting by then of 160 acres) for $3,000 in 1896. Around the turn of the century, they also constructed the house and barns with which I became acquainted as a child. The farmstead continued in the ownership of the Balzer family until my parents purchased it in 1948.

While all of Heinrich's and Katharina's surviving children lived nearby, many grandchildren did not remain in Minnesota. The primary exceptions were Jacob's children, most of whom stayed in the area, my grandmother Sarah included. About half of Peter's children also stayed.

Berry's Paternal Ratzlaff Line

Heinrich Ratzlaff grew up in a *Kleine Gemeinde* family. When he was 16 years old, his father died due to an infection in his hand. At age 18, young Heinrich moved with his mother and sister from Blumstein in Molotschna to the newly-established Borozenko Colony. At age 26 and with two children of his own, he and his wife sold their land, livestock and implements and immigrated to North America. Along with many others, they made their departure in May 1874.

The group Heinrich was part of traveled to Quebec because their final destination was Manitoba, Canada. There Heinrich played a key role in "spying out the land" and deciding to settle along the Scratching River near the present municipality of Morris, Manitoba. The settlers chose him as the first mayor of their little village, which they called Rosenort. Upon seeing the land near the Scratching River, he is said to have written the following words in German on the trunk of a dead tree. "It is good to be here, let us build our homes."

Strong family and religious ties connected the members of the Manitoba settlement with the *Kleine Gemeinde* group that settled in Nebraska and frequent letters kept the two groups apprised of life in the other location. The warmer weather and advantageous growing conditions in Nebraska powerfully attracted the Manitoba contingent. In 1875, just a year after settling in Manitoba, Heinrich and his immediate family relocated to Jefferson County, Nebraska and started over again. In his diary, he wrote this account of his first days there.

> "When we arrived June 14, we began from the beginning again . . . After we had visited here one week, my brother-in-law Klassen accompanied me to Fairbury to buy horses. After much questioning, we went to a farmer named Bondi who was eager to sell. We found 2 horses, one Wallach 3 years and the other 5 years. He sold them to me for $160 together; then two cows for $45 together, one buggy, harness, pails and a brush for $20, a total of $225. . . . I then bought a large wagon from Greeves, a crop of planted corn and wheat from an Englander. I also bought potatoes and garden vegetables, altogether 25 acres (of such) for $50.00. Now we were happy; we already had a harvest in 1875."[33]

Other Manitoba families joined the Ratzlaffs in Nebraska to escape the harsh winters. A trickle of other immigrants continued to arrive from Russia. By the end of 1877, around sixty Russian immigrant families were living in Jefferson County. Together, they established seven settlements, all in the Russian pattern of building sites closely situated along a common road with long, rectangular fields stretching behind.

Heinrich purchased his first Nebraska farmland from his uncle, Isaac Harms, on March 21, 1878. It was an 80 acre tract in Section 5 of Cub Creek Precinct, including the creek at its north end, and was conveyed for the below-market price of $300. The 1880 census provides details about the Ratzlaff farm. The value of the tract (55 acres improved and 25 acres unimproved) was pegged at $1,100. In addition to the two horses and two cows Heinrich referenced in his diary entry, Heinrich now owned two head of other cattle, two calves, two pigs and 25 chickens. Altogether, this livestock had a value of $250. He also owned farm implements having a value of $135 and an inventory of grain with a value of $200. On the land Heinrich raised barley (seven acres), Indian corn (seven acres), and wheat (forty acres).

In December 1881, Heinrich's wife died at age 31, leaving him the sole parent of five children. Always inclined to act quickly and decisively, by late February Heinrich had remarried. His bride was 22-year-old Elizabeth Flaming. Their first child and my grandmother, named Elizabeth after her mother, arrived a year later.

Heinrich was a dynamic individual and his contemporaries recognized him as a leader. Selected by the *Kleine Gemeinde* as a minister in 1885, he left that group in 1888 after a dispute with its elder, Abraham L. Friesen. He then joined what later became the *Bruderthaler* congregation, which ordained him to the ministry in November 1889.

Together, Heinrich and Elizabeth had twelve children, eleven of whom survived to adulthood and subsequently married. This large family scattered during the drought and depression of the thirties to other places, including Manitoba, California and Kansas.

Berry's Paternal Friesen Line

The Friesens began their long journey at Nikopol, near Borozenko Colony, where they boarded a steamship for the short voyage down the Dnieper River to the Black Sea and then west to the city of Odessa. From there, they traveled by train toward Berlin, perhaps via Budapest and Prague. After reaching Berlin, they proceeded to Hamburg where they boarded a ship to take them across the English Channel. Their next stop was Hull, along the east coast of England, where they disembarked and took a train to Liverpool. From there they made the Atlantic crossing to New York City where they disembarked July 17, 1874.

They traveled by train to Clarence Center, New York, where temporary lodging was available and the men found work with the harvest. The delay enabled three men to go ahead, view lands in Kansas and Nebraska, and make a final choice between them.

With Nebraska finally chosen, they boarded the train again for the final leg of their journey through Chicago and Omaha and to their destination in Beatrice.[34] This was the county seat of Gage County and just 20 miles east of the property they had decided to buy. The entire group stayed in Beatrice about one month until temporary buildings had been erected on their newly purchased lands in Jefferson County.

My great-grandfather, Gerhard, was part of this group and eleven years old at the time. With him on the journey were his father, Jacob L. Friesen; an uncle and aunt who had raised him, Abraham L. and Anna Friesen; his grandparents, Jacob W. and Aganetha Friesen; and his second cousin and future wife, Helena Friesen.

In its Sept. 10, 1874 edition, the *Beatrice Express* published this account of their arrival.

> "The colony here, which consists of 28 families, comprising about 120 souls, is now busily at work preparing to build on their lands in Jefferson County. . . They will build frame barns this fall, which they will use for dwellings through the winter, and next season will build substantial dwellings of brick and stone. They bought at St. Joseph (Missouri) about 5,000 feet of lumber, 53 horses, 87 head of oxen, 20 Studebaker wagons and a few other farming implements. The most of their smaller utensils, as well as supplies, they buy of Beatrice merchants. . . .
>
> "The lands brought by the Russians lie in town three, range three, Jefferson County, and although they have been given a few days more to make their individual selections, the whole tract bargained for amounts to 15,000 acres. This they got for $3.51 an acre, cash down, which is 40 percent off of the company's (Burlington and Missouri River Rail Road) usual cash rates. The lands, which are south of Cub Creek, have been described to us by residents of Jefferson County as first-class in soil and location. And the Russians themselves are entirely pleased with them.
>
> "The grasshopper situation does not discourage them in the least, which is a fact American newcomers should consider and ponder upon. They bring some money with them, which

helps to make a good start, but they are a hardworking, frugal class, and can manage to live and prosper under circumstances that would seem discouraging to our farmers."[35]

During that first winter in Nebraska, the immigrants finalized their land purchases. Although of mixed financial means, we shouldn't think of them as poor or destitute. When they arrived in Nebraska, some carried thousands of dollars in proceeds from farm sales back in Russia. To settlers already struggling to establish homesteads on bare land, the new Mennonite arrivals seemed rich.

That first winter, Jacob W. Friesen purchased 395 acres of bare land in sections 17 and 18 of Cub Creek Precinct for $1,302. Abraham L. Friesen, purchased 640 acres in those same two sections for around $2,150. By and large, this was level, well-drained ground with only gentle changes in elevation. Along the western 300 yards of Section 18 was a low area through which flowed one of the branches of Cub Creek. It was here they built their homes and barns, perhaps because of the close proximity of water and meadowland for the animals.

Ten years later, Gerhard's father bought 80 acres in Section 18. We don't know why he did not participate in the initial round of purchases. His first wife died in Russia after five years of marriage leaving him with four children. He may have had some difficulty finding a second wife. Compared to his brother, father, and grandfather, all of whom were *Kleine Gemeinde* leaders, Jacob L. Friesen appears not to have had public accomplishments. Most likely we will never know why.

*****

The stock market crash of 1929 had little immediate impact in Nebraska where investments tended toward tangible assets. But as the financial woes of the financial class deepened, access to capital became more limited and more expensive. This began to ripple across the United States, eventually causing many small rural banks to fail. Without access to capital, business began contracting and the Great Depression began.

Throughout the years after the migration of the *Kleine Gemeinde* to Kansas, my grandparents, George and Elizabeth Friesen, struggled to achieve a measure of financial stability and security. They started a small business in Jansen, farmed at three locations, and occupied at least five different residences. In 1932, with the purchase of a small farm and a wage-paying job at the creamery to supplement the farm income, George and Elizabeth prepared to endure the economic storm.

And then came the drought. Over the years the Friesens lived in Nebraska, rainfall averaged 30-35 inches annually. During the ten years from 1931 through 1940, annual rainfall was almost always below average and in five of those years, the annual total was around 20 inches.

With crops withering in the field and credit unavailable from the banks, farmers and businesses began to fail. Aunt Esther's husband, Nick Kroeker, recalled:

> "Everyone was broke. We had nothing because of the depression and the drought. Nearly everyone left. The Mennonite Brethren Church in Jansen closed as nearly all of its members were gone. We could live there with government help but there was no future, no identity in that."

Uncle Pete was the first to leave Nebraska, in 1935, to Delft, Minnesota and an opportunity to buy a grocery store. A year later, Uncle Henry left for Reedley, California and Aunt Lena for Bellingham, Washington. Uncle Herman toughed it out working for area farmers until 1938, when he too left for Delft; later he and his family moved again, this time to California.

Done with school at 14 and eager to make his way in the world, my father (John) went to Minnesota in the summer of 1935 when he was only 16. He lived in Delft with his brother, Pete, and worked for a local farmer. As noted earlier, there he met my mother.

Aunt Esther's decision to leave Nebraska had little to do with the depression or the drought. From an early age, she felt a calling to communicate the story of Jesus Christ as an international missionary. In 1939, she enrolled at St. Paul Bible College to prepare for her life's work. Soon after, she began dating Nick Kroeker, a student at Moody Bible Institute in Chicago who also was preparing himself for international mission. They married in 1941 and moved to West Africa (Mali) in 1946, where they lived and worked for nearly forty years.

Uncle Jack, the youngest member of the family, made his exit from Nebraska in 1940 at age 18. He lived and worked for a year in Mountain Lake and then moved to Reedley to take a grocery store job Uncle Henry had arranged. After Pearl Harbor, he was inducted into the army where he served as a medical corpsman.

Last to leave Nebraska were my grandparents, George and Elizabeth. In 1939, they lost their residence and farm due to their default in the mortgage to the Federal Land Bank of Omaha. Out of farming for the first time since 1918, George began operating a filling station in Jansen. In the spring of 1941, they moved to Mountain Lake where he again operated a filling station.

Grandpa was not happy in Mountain Lake with the cold winter weather, the absence of life-long friends and community standing, and his and Grandma's poor financial prospects. In February, 1944, after three years in Mountain Lake, they sold most of their belongings at a public sale and moved to California. Grandma died in 1948 at age 65; Grandpa died in 1954 at age 69. I have no memories of either of them.

Looking at this family line and all the moves its members made, I understand why my father often dreamed of California. Nice as it was in Minnesota, he had always perceived it as but another stop along the way.

From Minnesota to Pennsylvania

Sharon and I grew up in a community surrounded by relatives and friends who also were part of our congregation. By and large, we interacted with the same people all seven days of the week. We believed the same things, understood lived experience in common terms, followed the same routines involving work and worship, and shared similar aspirations. The authority of God stood behind it all.

This sort of fully integrated life, where what fits and what does not fit is based on authoritative religious assumptions, is what sociologists often refer to as a "sacred canopy." Life under the sacred canopy is coherent; it makes sense. Choices may be comparatively few but when someone asks the question, "Why do you do this or do that?" the answer is clear and readily available. Because such a life is coherent, it has the power to endure and is generally respected by outsiders, even if they are not persuaded to become part of it.

While much of our lives as children fits this metaphor, it also is important to acknowledge that already during our childhoods the canopy was torn and tattered. Most of Mom's brothers and sisters no longer lived according to the expectations of the Carson Mennonite Brethren Church and yet we happily socialized with them whenever Mom could arrange an event. Sharon had a similar experience in her family, where some of the Klassen cousins lived very different lives than she and her siblings. Because we did not shun family members who failed to conform, we exposed ourselves to the need to account for the differences among us. This same dynamic was present at school, especially after we finished grade school in Delft and began attending the larger school in Mountain Lake.

Though tattered, the canopy was still in place for Sharon and me, at least during the 1950s. But it never was part of our daughters' reality and in this respect their lives marked a departure from several centuries of family history. They were raised in crowded places surrounded by strangers who held diverse assumptions about life. They experienced much less consensus and encountered many more choices. When they asked why we did this or that, as often as not our answers seemed arbitrary. When their family of origin engaged in practices that differed from the families of their friends and neighbors, they felt confusion as often as pride.

In short, they are the first generation in our family to not have experienced the security and shelter of a sacred canopy.

Sharon and I have always perceived ourselves to be a transition generation that needed to establish new patterns to replace the old. Yes, we welcomed the opportunity to experience greater diversity, to have the freedom to express skepticism, to have more choices. But especially with the arrival of Amber and Emily, we began to focus on the challenge of providing a pathway that would lead them to the faith and the commitments we had received from our parents. We found ourselves looking again for the coherence of shared assumptions and embodied faith. It wasn't to be found there in St. Paul where we were living.

It's silly to imagine one can stitch together a sacred canopy after it has been rent and dispersed by the winds of change. Such a task requires generations of intense community living around shared beliefs. So how do parents who appreciate the tradition in which they were raised proceed with family life in an urban, more secular setting?

In December 1981, when our daughters were five and three, we made our first serious attempt to assemble a life that had some of the features of our youth. We bought a 3-story duplex in a run-down block of the Seward neighborhood in Minneapolis. Across the back alley were several large houses owned by a slumlord with rooms rented by-the-week. But across the street were the meeting house where our congregation worshipped on Sundays and the house where our pastor, Myron Schrag, and his family lived. Also across the street were the neighborhood school and community center. Members of our congregation lived nearby, including one who managed the community center.

At the same time we moved to Seward, three other members of our home fellowship group bought houses just one block away. And we rented the upper unit of our house to three young Mennonite Central Committee (MCC) volunteers who had been assigned to the St. Paul/Minneapolis area; that brought more like-minded role models into our children's lives.

One evening each week, our fellowship group met in one of our homes for an evening of singing, conversation and prayer. Friday evenings we'd host a neighborhood potluck, Saturdays we occasionally shared work, Sunday always involved at least one meeting at the church. Amber and Emily participated in all of these activities.

Those years in the early '80s were among the best of our lives; the passage of time has not tarnished the memories at all. Yet in retrospect, they rested on a fragile base of supports. Over time, key participants moved out of the neighborhood. People married, others divorced. We had disagreements within our home fellowship group. Relationships changed and the novelty wore off. None of it was wrenching or even surprising; it was just the normal stuff of life pushing at us.

As our community experienced the normal wear-and-tear of living, we began to lose the confidence that our children would grow into their teenage years with an understanding of embodied, communal Christian faith. Instead, we feared, they would conclude that religious faith is a mish-mash of magical beliefs one pastes together in order to cope with life's difficulties.

During the early '80s, I discovered the writings of Stanley Hauerwas, the Christian ethicist. Ethics, he said, is first and foremost about who we are as a people. The community of which we are a part teaches us how to see the world and how to encounter life. If it provides us with a truthful account of the world, Hauerwas wrote, then we are prepared to respond to ethical challenges in a life-giving way. Without such a community and its equipping role, even a so-called Christian ethic becomes arbitrary and unworthy of our trust.[36]

We took this very seriously. But though we were trying, creating an enduring, truthful community in the city was no easy thing. Life in Seward continued to be good, but we also knew we likely would never recover the coherence of those few golden years.

Meanwhile, I was practicing law with a civil legal aid firm in St. Paul. It wasn't a plum job in financial terms, but it was coveted work because we occasionally litigated important cases that ended up helping many people. And the firm I worked for had an excellent reputation, in part because it included some of the best lawyers in the Twin Cities area.

As the years went by, I became aware that increasingly I went to work each day hoping to pick up "an interesting case" that would have a broad impact. My aspirations were fine, but such cases are not routine in the life of a legal aid attorney. What is routine is a waiting room filled with prospective clients and 100 open case-files in the drawer. If I wasn't motivated by the routine work, maybe it was time to move on.

Another important dynamic during this period related to our congregation, Faith Mennonite Church, a group jointly affiliated with the General Conference Mennonites and the (Old) Mennonite Church. We loved that congregation and admired many of the people we worshipped with there, but it was small and the membership in constant flux. We doubted our daughters would have a group of steady companions there during their teenage years. Then there was the tendency of adults in the congregation to fasten their attention and energy on specific ethical issues, especially those linked to sexuality. In these characteristics, Faith Mennonite was like many other urban congregations.

Our need, as we saw it then, was for less emphasis on our questions and more on our affirmations, less emphasis on innovation and more on tradition. We no more wanted our daughters to think faith to be an amalgam of politically correct opinions than we wanted them to think of it as a magical realm. But unless they were part of a group of people living in a counter-cultural way because of their commitment to the way of Jesus, those were the two religious approaches most likely to shape their understanding of faith.

During those years, Sharon and I often had contact with staff from MCC because its service workers lived in the apartment upstairs. In '85, we interviewed for the position of "MCC country representative" in the Philippines and in '88, I interviewed for an executive role. When called in early 1989 and invited to give leadership to MCC's Service Program in the United States, Sharon encouraged me to say "yes." I did.

As we imagined it then, a part of the sacred canopy was still in place in Lancaster. It had stable congregations and a 275-year-old Mennonite community large enough to be very public in its witness. We wouldn't need to stitch something together. And the visible, physical presence of a community of faith would help us all better understand what following Jesus is all about.

Did we find what we had hoped for? Some of it. Our Lancaster congregation, East Chestnut Street Mennonite Church, had a stronger consensus around core assumptions than we had experienced in Minneapolis. It had more children, a more vibrant youth program, and the opportunity for Amber and Emily to spend time with families who were deeply rooted in faith and tradition. The wider community included many Mennonites in public and private roles. All around us were the Amish, a group that embodied in their traditional ways an understanding of life that elevated the communal over the personal.

Still, as we had done in Minneapolis, we deliberately lived in a city neighborhood and sought opportunities for Amber and Emily to get acquainted with children from other religious and cultural backgrounds. We hedged our commitment to tradition by encouraging them to attend public schools rather than private Mennonite schools. Yes, we wanted the reassurance of that sacred canopy, but the experience of the strong Mennonite presence in Lancaster County also caused a bit of ambivalence to surface. It was most comfortable for us over by the edge, where we also could see the blue sky.

Carson in March

I try to imagine their lives here
unsheltered from winter's wind
fixed on farm, faith and family
far removed from the world at large.

I could have done that too;
it would have been my home
had I stayed on this snow-ribbed ground
the challenges tactile and tangible,
Wienses and Balzers sleeping nearby.
It was here for me, a gift I declined
in pursuit of a better world
inhabited by perfect strangers.

Still, I can't say it's finished;
this place holds me yet in its spell
conjuring a constant reminder:
honor, trust, step up, do well.

[1] Berry, Wendell. "The Futility of Global Thinking," *Harper's Magazine,* September 1989 at 16-22.

[2] Well into the 20th century, relevant real estate documents used the traditional spelling: Klaassen. Sometime during the '30s or '40s, one "a" was dropped. Because it is more familiar among current members of the extended family, I have used the modern version throughout this work.

[3] *Seventy-Five Years in Minnesota,* published by the Mennonite churches of Mountain Lake in 1950. This excerpt is by H.E. Wiens.

[4] *Jublilee Celebration – The Mennonite Settlement in Mountain Lake, Minnesota 1875-1925,* published by Mennonite churches of Mountain Lake in 1925; republished by Heritage Village in 2000.

[5] Vangie and Ron Patrick's two children are Damon and Derek.

[6] Physicians, engineers, administrators, inventors, and scholars were among the alumni of the two congregations. To cite just one example, academic leadership, these congregations nurtured four college presidents (J.N.C. Hiebert, Tabor College, 1952-53; B.J. Braun, Pacific Bible Institute, 1947-50 and Mennonite Brethren Biblical Seminary, 1955-62; Silas Bartsch, and D. Merrill Ewert, Fresno Pacific College/University, 1982-83 and 2005-present respectively) and two academic deans (John Fadenrecht, Wheaton College during the 1950s and Waldo Hiebert, Mennonite Brethren Biblical Seminary during the '70s and '80s). Arthur J. Wiebe, President of Fresno Pacific College 1950-65, Kenneth Janzen, Dean of Hamline University during the '80s and '90s, and Clarence Hiebert, President of Tabor College in 1994-95, were sons of parents who grew up in these congregations.

[7] Ratzlaff, Kenneth L. *Grandma's Window,* California Mennonite Historical Society, 2004. Given Russian Mennonite clannishness, it may be more impressive to find someone not related to this couple.

[8] vander Zijpp, Nanne. "Zijbrandt Claesz (d. 1535)." *Global Anabaptist Mennonite Encyclopedia Online,* 1959.

[9] Neff, Christian. "Jan Claesz (d. 1544)." *Global Anabaptist Mennonite Encyclopedia Online,* 1957.

[10] van Braght, Thieleman J. *Martyrs' Mirror of the Defenseless Christians,* Herald Press, 1950, at 471.

[11] Id., at 831.

[12] Id., at 979.

[13] van der Zijpp, Nanne and C. F. Brüsewitz. "Netherlands." *Global Anabaptist Mennonite Encyclopedia Online.*, 1987.

[14] Krahn, Cornelius, Nanne van der Zijpp and James M. Stayer. "Münster Anabaptists." *Global Anabaptist Mennonite Encyclopedia Online,* 1987.

[15] Quoted in Klassen, Peter J. *Mennonites in Early Modern Poland & Prussia,* The Johns Hopkins University Press, 2009, at 32.

[16] Penner, Horst and Peter J. Foth. "West Prussia." *Global Anabaptist Mennonite Encyclopedia Online,* 1989.

[17] Bangs, Jeremy D. *Friesens and Cousins, A Baltic Past,* self-published, 1980. Concerning Bernhard von Riesen, whose portrait was painted in 1521 by the German master, Albrecht Durer, Bangs notes the name indicated his family came from the land of Riesen near Marienburg (Poland). While the Friesen name appears to have come from the Netherlands, Bangs cautions against attaching too much to the distinction between the Prussian von Riesens and the Dutch Friesens. "Whatever the origin of all the people named von Riesen and Friesen, the group was practically closed by 1600 and for two centuries the Friesens, Wiebes, van Clouwenhovens, von Riesens, Eidzes (or von Eidzens or perhaps Edzemas) married each other (and) moved within the friendly, bickering circles of Mennonites only. By 1800 there could not have been a single von Riesen or Friesen in the *Werder* unrelated to others of the same name. They had become one family." Id. at 16-17.

[18] Balzer, Waldo and Alvin Balzer. *The Wonderful Story of the Balzers,* self-published 1989, at 22.

[19] The "t" in Baltzer was dropped during the years living in Russia.

[20] Klassen, *Mennonites in Early Modern Poland & Prussia*, 197.

[21] Krahn, Cornelius and Walter W. Sawatsky. "Russia." *Global Anabaptist Mennonite Encyclopedia Online,* 1989.

[22] Urry, James. "Land Distribution (Russia)." *Global Anabaptist Mennonite Encyclopedia Online,* 1989.

[23] Klassen, John. *Testing Faith & Tradition,* Good Books, 2006, at 189.

[24] Krahn, Cornelius. "Molotschna Mennonite Settlement (Zaporizhia Oblast, Ukraine)." *Global Anabaptist Mennonite Encyclopedia Online,* 1957.

[25] Plett, Delbert F. *Saints and Sinners – The Kleine Gemeinde in Imperial Russia,* Crossway Publications, 1999, at 74-77.

[26] Id. at 261.

[27] Loewen, Royden K. *Family Church, and Market: A Mennonite Community in the Old and New Worlds, 1850-1930,* University of Illinois Press, 1993 at 19-30.

[28] Plett, supra, at 113-7.

[29] Krahn, Cornelius and Adolf Ens. "Manitoba (Canada)." *Global Anabaptist Mennonite Encyclopedia Online,* 1989.

[30] Reimer, Gustav E. and G.R. Gaeddert. *Exiled by the Czar: Cornelius Jansen and the Great Mennonite Migration of 1874,* Mennonite Publication Office, 1956.

[31] Friesen, J. John and Cornelius Krahn. "Mountain Lake Minnesota." *Global Anabaptist Mennonite Encyclopedia Online,* 1957.

[32] Wiebe, Orlando H. "Schultz, Peter (1853-1930)." *Global Anabaptist Mennonite Encyclopedia Online,* 1959.

[33] Heinrich Ratzlaff's diary is published in *Profile of the Mennonite Kleine Gemeinde 1874,* DFP Publications, 1987, at 187-192.

[34] For a fuller account of these events, see Friesen, Berry, "The Nebraska Roots of the Descendants of George A. Friesen and Elizabeth Ratzlaff" in *Preservings 2008,* D.F. Plett Historical Research Foundation, at 50.

[35] Quoted in *Profile of the Mennonite Kleine Gemeinde 1874* at 97.

[36] Hauerwas, Stanley. *Peaceable Kingdom: A Primer in Christian Ethics,* University of Notre Dame Press, 1983.

"God calls you to where your deep gladness and the world's deep hunger meet."[1]

Frederick Buechner

Chapter 2: How will we make a living?

Our physical needs press in upon us day by day, even hour by hour, and there is no escape from their demands. And so we marshal our time and energy, inventory our most desirable skills and aptitudes, and ponder how to earn our daily bread. Other needs also come into play, such as dignity, character, and human companionship. Making a living brings this all together while pushing us into the broader world to collide and collaborate with others. The possibilities are many; this chapter describes a few that members of our families have pursued.

On the Farm

In my favorite memories of Dad, he's working. I'm a boy of seven or eight at his side. He's dressed in his overalls and ankle-high work shoes with a brimmed cap on his head to shield his eyes from the sun. He's walking fast with Trix (our dog) and me running to keep up; our destination isn't clear, but it involves fixing a fence, preparing the barn for chickens or readying the combine for harvest. What specifically he'll be doing isn't that important; he just loves to work. I can tell because he's whistling as he walks, a sure sign all is well with the world.

Dad was a farmer who enjoyed his job. Only it wasn't a job exactly; no one told him what to do each day and no one gave him a paycheck at week's end. It was more like a business with cash flow projections, serious meetings with the banker, and timing the sale of farm produce to hit the top of the market. Yet that doesn't exactly fit either because most of all, farming involved a place to raise a family.

Yet Dad started married life working for a paycheck. When first married in 1939, Dad worked for an electrician wiring barns and houses. That winter, he caught on as a sales clerk with a Mountain Lake grocer. Apparently he had the ability to engage customers and deal with the public. Sometime later in 1940, the local Ford dealer hired him to sell cars and trucks.

For reasons we don't fully understand, in the fall of 1941 he made his move into farming, just like generations of Friesen men before him. Part of his motivation may have been military conscription. The United States Congress enacted draft legislation in September 1940. Although the draft did not become fully operational until later, Dad was certainly aware that conscription was coming and might include him. Writing in 1982, Mom recalled that "John would have liked to stay there [Wolf Motor Company], but there was a war going on and he wanted to get on a farm to avoid the draft."

Mom's diary of October 28, 1941 includes this entry.

> "Today noon Johnny came home and said that he could get a place on a farm for next spring if he could get somebody to live in the place during the winter months. He is going to ask (his) folks but I doubt they'll want to move now since they have rented out their rooms. Johnny has talked farm for quite a while already. I hope we can get the place since that's where he wants to be. I guess LeeRoy and I could learn to be farmers too if we tried hard enough."

In early March 1942, just weeks after Marley was born in Mountain Lake, they moved to the Moffet farm northeast of Delft. Dad's parents had been wrecked financially by the Great Depression and had no money to help Dad get started. Mom's parents helped some with equipment and labor. Carl Wolf, Dad's former employer at the Ford dealership, provided a loan, enabling him to acquire his first team of horses to do the plowing. He planted 80 acres of corn that first spring. They also had about 75 laying hens for eggs and four cows. Mom wrote, "It really is swell to have eggs and cream!"

Though raised on a farm and well-acquainted with the demands of farming life, Mom didn't love to work the way Dad did. Mom loved to read. Work she tolerated, but it didn't give her joy.

Mom said she and Dad quarreled about work, especially at first on the farm, but off-and-on again throughout their 32 years of married life. "Dad wanted me to help him outside, in addition to the cooking and the baking and the canning and the washing and the housework and the children," Mom would say. She'd make it sound unreasonable, but we both knew plenty of women who did all of that and still helped with outside work. The thing was, those other women didn't read. For Mom, life without books was an impoverished existence!

Actually, I think Dad and Mom were basically at peace about this after a while. Theirs was a marriage built on the attractiveness of difference and this was one of their differences.

During that first year of farming on the Moffet farm, Dad's energy and affability won the attention of Jim Redding, the Bingham Lake banker. Redding owned a farm and needed a tenant. Mom wrote this account of that second farm.

> "We wanted to move away from Mr. Moffet. It was not easy living in his house [with him upstairs]. John started looking for a place and was led to the Redding farm east of the church where we could farm fifty-fifty with everything. Mr. Redding, the banker in Bingham Lake, made us an offer and we accepted.
>
> "We moved there March 1, 1943. It was our fifth move. The house was better and we had twelve cows to start with. Half belonged to Mr. Redding, the other half he [lent] us. Here we got our first tractor and other machinery. And we worked that way for two and one-half years, everything fifty-fifty. We raised chickens. That was my job. We bought a milking machine that had to be run by a motor; we still had no electricity. I learned to run the milker too. When John was harvesting, I had to do more chores."

LeRoy has clear memories of living on the Redding farm. Here is his description of a few of those memories, starting with the evening ritual of going to the pasture with Mom and Marley to get the cows.

"We would walk out to the large stone north of the barn and then turn west moving along the cornfield and then into a pasture area up against some woods on the far side which contained an abandoned house. Often Dad would be working in the fields and we were to get the cows into the barn ready for him to milk when he came in. We would set out for the pasture while it was yet light often coming back amid the soft, moist darkness of dusk with its harsh mosquitoes.

"Especially during evenings around the summer solstice when the pinks and blues and oranges and charcoals would go on forever and ever, I experienced feelings and moods for which I still have no words. I remember these trips to the pasture as usually leisurely with time spent around the rock, time spent calling to the cows ("come bas, come bas") rather than rounding them up and chasing them home.

"It was a perfect time for stories. My mother, yet in her mid-twenties at the time, was seemingly always eager to tell stories. She was a romantic, a person who loved old fashioned (as she called them) stories, whether found in books or in her own family of origin. I liked to get her going. By the time I began school several years later, I had some acquaintance with much of the fiction my mother loved to read, and I knew a great deal about the growing-up experiences of my mother and her seven siblings.

"The four girls in Louise May Alcott's novels were often houseguests. My mother liked Meg best. Such stories might be told in the garden of flowers and vegetables just south of the house; they might be told on the round rock as the sun slipped behind the woods off to the west and the altered ethos of a hot and humid summer night settled in; they might be told as we huddled around the cob fire in the kitchen amid a raging blizzard outside. The ease of hearing stories from, and later telling them to, my mother would remain alive and well throughout all of the changes of childhood, adolescence and adulthood."

In October 1945, my parents moved yet again to become tenants on the 200-acre Balzer farm, the place Mom's great-grandparents had first settled 69 years earlier. The house was connected to the electrical grid and had a cistern to catch rain water. Mom rejoiced at the convenience on her first wash day. There they made their living until Dad died, twenty-six years later.

When we consider this matter of "making a living," it would be a mistake to think only of money they obtained through the sale of farm products. For those of us who depend on paychecks, money mostly describes what making a living entails. But for Mom and Dad, it involved many activities that never were monetized. A lot of one's living came out of the garden or out of the barn in the form of eggs, milk, and meat. Some of it required special skills, such as sewing, fixing a broken machine, or constructing a shed. Some of it involved barter and the exchange of labor and equipment with others.

So the sources of one's sustenance were varied and only a portion involved cash. Thus, a day Mom spent mending clothes, butchering chickens, and canning garden vegetables had significant value, but never showed up in any accounting ledger.

Dad was a good farmer. He made many improvements to the farm, including a new granary, new foundations under the barn and machine shed, and drainage tile under low-lying land. His fences were tight, his rows straight, his machinery well-maintained, and his harvests out of the field before the winter snows. But looking back now with my own working years mostly behind me, it strikes me that he never made a full commitment to farming. The 80 acres he and Mom bought in 1947 was the extent of their investment in land. In later years they could have increased their holdings, but it never came up. During the late '40s and early '50s, Dad always had a small dairy operation on the farm. But when dairy inspectors began raising standards for the on-farm cooling of the milk, Dad sold the cows rather than investing in a cooling tank.

Early in 1957, he began selling farm equipment (New Holland, New Idea, Allis Chambers, Minneapolis Moline) for Penner Implement in Mountain Lake. Later, he sold cars and trucks for Regehr Chevrolet. Farming gradually became mostly a matter of seeding the land in the spring and harvesting the crop in the fall. We boys did the summer work, thereby earning our college tuition and extending our time at home.

I've often wondered about Dad's less than whole-hearted commitment to farming. Perhaps it reflected his worries about his heart and its capacity to sustain him through the rigors of farm work. His return to sales work in Mountain Lake followed close on the heels of a bout of chest pain the previous fall, when he was only 38 years old. The timing suggests those two events may have been related.

Or perhaps Dad's ambivalence about farming had been there all along. He had started his married life working for employers in town. During the years when he was a full-time farmer, his trips to area towns (Delft, Bingham Lake, Mountain Lake, Windom) were many. Reading some of Mom's diary entries during the '40s and '50s leaves one wondering who really was working harder, Mom with her books doing the inside work or Dad out-of-doors dashing off to town whenever the opportunity arose. At least part of his motivation for all those trips to town must have been social.

At any rate, during the last twelve or so years of his too-short life, Dad made much of his living in town, working with people and earning a commission. He became widely known across Cottonwood County as a Chevrolet salesman. He was very good at it. Like his father before him, Dad appreciated nice cars and he enjoyed trying to sell them. He was honest as the day is long and consistently cheerful and good-humored, even as he honed the art of making the deal. What's not to like about a salesman like that?

There was a down side. He had a grumpy boss who seemed to dislike a man who whistled while he worked. By working for a paycheck, he lost some of his independence as well as the esteem a rural community grants only serious and successful farmers. But all in all, I imagine Dad was happy with the balance he found between his work on the farm and his work in town.

And Mom? She liked it too. With Dad in town, the farm was less hectic and she could schedule her work and her reading with fewer interruptions from her beloved Johnny.

*****

Looking back through the roster of my male ancestors, I first see 250 years of farmers. But when I look more closely, I see many of the men made a living through a mix of activities pursued either consecutively or at the same time.

Grandpa Friesen farmed in Jefferson County Nebraska. But he also employed his skills as a smithy and a mechanic. Aunt Esther recalls that during the '20s, he had a forge on the farm they were renting and took in work, such as hammering out plowshares. He also hired himself out as a mechanic for the huge, steam-driven grain threshers that operated in Nebraska during those years.

As a younger man, Grandpa and his brother operated a mechanical repair shop out of a shed they purchased in the town of Jansen. I imagine them working as "motor-heads" for that first generation of automobile owners.

Great-grandfather Ratzlaff also farmed in Jefferson County. And he was a minister, first in the *Kleine Gemeinde* congregation and then in the *Bruderthaler* congregation near Jansen. I assume neither of those congregations paid him for his work, but he probably received support in the form of gifts from the members.

Great-grandfather Wiens farmed in Cottonwood County and was a minister too. The male members of the Mennonite Brethren (MB) Church first elected him in 1883 and the national MB Conference ordained him in 1885. He served in that capacity until 1916. Again, he received some material benefit from this work, although I doubt that he perceived it to be a beneficial economic arrangement.

Abraham J. Wiebe, Sharon's great-uncle, followed a similar pattern as he was a farmer who also served as lead minister for the Carson MB congregation from 1916 until 1939.

Plying a Trade or a Skill

On the list of outstanding Mennonite achievements, the first is their demonstration that allegiance to God takes priority over allegiance to the state. We see evidence of this achievement today in the wide acceptance of the need for separation of church from state and the broad support for freedom of conscience, although that is not the language the Anabaptists and early Mennonites would have used to describe it.

Second on the list of achievements is draining the lowlands of the Vistula Delta in Poland.

During the years 1547-1550, the drainage effort was launched across a 30-40 mile arc from Danzig in the west to Lake Drausen just south of Elbing in the east. Just about all of this land lay several feet below sea level.

To begin, the land was divided into sections and leased to drainage associations. An association, which consisted of area farmers and laborers, would first build a dike around its area so they had some degree of control over what occurred within that area. It also would negotiate agreements with adjoining associations so water expelled from one area could be managed as it passed toward the Baltic Sea. This required accurate calibrations of ground levels.

Within each area, the drainage associations built wind pumps at the lowest point. The wind pumps, which looked like windmills but did not grind grain, lifted the water from the protected fields and deposited it in outlet channels. Because the land was very flat, side channels also were cut into the land to guide the water to the wind pumps. Between the side channels, the land was leveled so water drained to a channel and did not sit on the land.

All land had to be cleared of bushes and swamp grass. This was handwork, of course, as was the dike building, canal digging, and leveling of land. It also was highly communal activity; members of a drainage association were jointly responsible for the entire area.

Swamp fever was a terrible scourge in the beginning. According to one report, nearly 80 percent of the first Mennonite settlers working in the marshes died from it.[2]

From swamp land to frequently-flooded pasture land took three or four generations of labor. Then dairy production began and along with it, cheese-making. *Werder* cheese became a well-known and sought-after product. On land that was a bit higher, wheat and rape seed were planted. These grain fields also provided a place where the cattle manure could be productively discarded.

Because flooding was assumed and continued even after all of this work was well underway, farmers attempted to construct their farm building on land above sea level. Such land generally was not available and so broad earthen mounds would be created to raise the ground level. Faced with the task of moving large volumes of dirt by hand, farmers had very small farmyards. The house and stable were built under one roof with a barn at a right angle at the far end of the stable. The corner area between the barn and the house served as the yard.

It wasn't just Mennonites who did this work; Catholics and Lutherans also were very involved. However, the Dutch immigrants had more of the required experience and so Mennonites generally provided leadership to the drainage associations.

*****

Among Sharon's ancestors we don't find many farmers (although her great-great-grandfather Gerhard Klassen was a farmer after he settled in Minnesota). Instead, at least with Sharon's father and grandfather, we find an emphasis on carpentry and woodworking. We don't have information about how the Klassens made a living during the Russian interlude. The fact that her great-great-grandfather Gerhard was born in Elbing, Prussia seems to suggest his father lived in a city, not the countryside, and was a tradesman, not a farmer. During the latter part of the 18th century, Prussian Mennonites developed a strong furniture-making tradition. It focused on household items for newly married couples (dowry furniture) and also on chests for transporting goods during the migration to Russia. Perhaps this is the line of work the Klassens performed before emigrating themselves after most of the other Mennonites had already left.

Notably, Sharon's great-grandmother, Elizabeth Voth Klassen Flaming, served the Mountain Lake community as a midwife for many years and received payment for her skill and efforts.

*****

Our memories of Sharon's father are fixed on his achievements as a lumber merchant and worker with wood. We have simply assumed he was at peace about following his father into the building trades. Yet journal entries Will wrote at age 23 reveal a struggle to reconcile himself to this path. At that age, he still was waiting to discover his vocation.

> "I think I'm learning a special lesson these days. When I was younger [and] before I was converted, I had a desire to be converted so that I would have special guidance in selecting my vocation or life's work. Now I have often recalled that desire, but I seem to be as lost as I was then.
>
> "It seems to be a definite instinct, a hereditary instinct, of our family, a certain inability to decide certain issues with definite decisiveness. Others have been able to say from high school on, 'I'm going to do this' and for that they prepare.
>
> "I have failed shamefully in that respect and now it seems God has to take so much time in order to bring me to the correct frame of mind and that is what I seem to be learning. To trust him and as he leads follow. Yes, I have often read that, but it seems certain things have to be experienced before they can be believed.

> "Things seem to shape themselves [such as] I will not have a steady job this summer, I will not be tied down in Mt. Lake next fall. Is he going to call me away? The very thought that perhaps he will be able to use me in a special way, that I will have a definite work which I know is what he chooses for me, is a happiness in itself. What it will be, I don't know and I'm going to try to be neutral, to have him place me. Then I'll know; here is where I belong. What a pillar of comfort that must have been for many a man already, 'God wants me here.'
>
> "Why so concerned anyhow? Does life need me that badly or is life this way that it comes without trying so hard for? No, life is plenty serious. As the wind, as the stream, it comes, it goes, and after it has passed, it is past. We are placed very near the tragic point. We reach it while still young, and how we act, what we take when, this is what will determine our way.
>
> "Mere existence is the condition of a great portion of man, but there are only few who are starting a heaven here amid these trials and hard luck ways."

When Sharon and I were dating, her mother, Esther, occasionally invited me to join a family meal. After we'd eaten, Will typically would begin talking about what was on his mind. Usually, the topic was a value he wanted us to emulate or an aspect of Christian theology he wanted to shore up. Perhaps the manner of his homilies reflected his underlying sense that he was meant to be a teacher. In my memory, however, he had indeed found his calling: a main street businessman with heart.

He often spoke of work and how to make a living. "Identify something that people need and then offer it at a fair price," he would say. "That's genuine service." He understood this to be what he and Esther did by operating Klassen Lumber Company. "We don't focus on making money," he'd say. And if he sensed a whiff of skepticism around the table, he'd belabor the point. "Yes, the businessman must make a living if he is to continue. But the heart of the matter is to offer a service at a fair price. If you do that, the profit will come."

Customer-centered service; that's what we'd call it now. Will was passionate about it. And he and Esther put long hours in the business to make it all happen in a sustainable way.

If we remained at the dinner table long enough, Will would begin to ruminate about a favorite sub-theme: employment practices. He relished the opportunity to employ people who needed a break. Usually, six or seven men worked as employees of the lumber yard as sales clerks, estimators, truss fabricators, delivery drivers, and/or carpenters. A couple were long-term and salaried while the rest worked for an hourly wage. Will had a penchant for hiring the guy who was on the wagon or who faced jail time if he didn't come up with a job. Will took a fair bit of criticism about this from his long-term employees because it hurt the productivity of his work force and left the experienced workers with more responsibility. But as he kept saying, it's not about the money, it's about the service. That word covered a lot of ground with him.

The biggest tension for Will and Esther as business owners had to do with the balance between work and church-and-family. Usually, that's how it would be said, with the three words "church-and-family" strung together as one thing. Sharon's mom was more apt to bring this up, perhaps because Will found it a bit uncomfortable to talk about.

By and large, Sharon's family regularly participated in nearly all church events. Sometimes the dynamics of the family spilled right out in the open at church, such as the Wednesday night prayer meeting when Will stood, requested prayer for his children, and then described in some detail the quarreling among them all through supper that evening. By bringing the children to church, Sharon's parents understood themselves to be engaging in another aspect of family life. Sharon recalls not always appreciating this approach. Working morning until evening and then being present every time the church was open made for very full days.

But everyone had a decent amount of face time with mom and dad. Will ate lunch and supper at home nearly every day and the family would be together then. Mary and Paul often worked at the lumber yard and saw their dad there. The family always had a big garden and that provided plenty of opportunities for Esther to work alongside her children. No one ever worked on Sundays, which freed up an entire day for a slower pace. Going to church together, eating together, and working together; that's how they lived out the fact that family life was one of their highest values

*****

In the congregation of our youth, being a missionary was the most highly regarded vocation of all. I'm referring here to those who went to live in another country, far from home and the support of family, to share the story of Jesus Christ with people who had never heard it before.

International missionaries gave up a lot and faced high odds of early death. In the congregation in which Sharon and I grew up, these individuals were heroes, equal to or exceeding the Anabaptist martyrs of the 16th century. In fact, we heard very little about the Anabaptist martyrs, but we heard lots about the missionaries. When they visited our community during their occasional travel to the United States, we would pack the meeting house to hear their stories and look at their pictures.

During the 60 years from 1896 until 1956, the two Mennonite Brethren congregations from Cottonwood County commissioned 29 missionaries (including five to serve within the U. S.).[3] This was a source of pride and our Sunday school teachers gently nudged us to consider joining their number. During our most fervent religious moments, most of us thought, "Yes, maybe God is calling me too."

Henry and Marie Ewert Enns were the first to be commissioned and were sent to Cameroon, West Africa in late 1896. There they died of tropical illnesses only six months after arriving. With the support of the Mennonite Brethren Conference, in 1899 the two congregations sent two other members, Nicholas and Susanna Wiebe Hiebert, to India. They returned soon after due to illness.

Mom had strong family connections to this bold and often costly enterprise. Mom's dad was a first cousin of Anna Suderman, the first Mennonite Brethren missionary from the United States to serve in India (1898) and resident there for 48 years.[4] Her mother's first cousins included two of the pioneers noted above, Henry Enns and Susanna Wiebe Hiebert, as well as Sara Balzer, commissioned to work among the American Indians. Mom's second cousins included missionaries J.N.C. Hiebert (India), Art Wiens (Italy), Ruth Wiens (Japan) and Robert Wiens (West Africa).

Mom's great-aunt, Maria Balzer Wiebe, in addition to being the mother of both Henry Ens and Susanna Wiebe Hiebert, began in 1888 to organize local "sewing circles" for the support of missionaries. It appears to have been the first such activity among Mennonite Brethren in the United States. The handiwork produced by the women in these sewing groups was sold each July 4th at auctions held in community buildings or on the church grounds. Such events, which featured food items and hand-made products from carpentry shops as well hand-sewn items, kept international missions high on the agenda throughout the year.

Dad's sister, Esther Kroeker, served as a lifelong missionary in Mali, West Africa. Aunt Esther and Uncle Nick often were in our home during their return trips from Mali, where two of their children died due in part to the lack of readily available medical care. They were engaging and energetic, quick with stories and jokes, knowledgeable about exotic practices and places, creative and adventurous and filled with passion for the emerging congregations of Christians in Mali. Their intensity and focus frightened but also attracted me. While I couldn't imagine myself a missionary, I admired their strong sense of purpose and their participation in work that seemed transformative for the people of Mali.

Sharon's family had strong missionary connections too. Her grandmother Eytzen was a half-sister of Suzanne Wiebe Hiebert. John A. Wiebe, who served in India from 1927 until 1963, was a first cousin of Sharon's mom. So was J.N.C. Hiebert, who also served in India. Sharon recalls conversations with her mother about being a missionary; these occurred while playing with her mom's button box and various shaped, sized and colored buttons Sharon would imagine to be people. In the words of the Sunday school song, "Red and yellow, black and white, all are precious in his sight. Jesus loves the little children of the world."

It's difficult to gauge the impact of these people and this tradition on our lives. It never resulted in serious thought on my part of becoming a missionary. But I think it fair to say that people held up before us as heroes when we are children shape us more strongly than we know. Missionaries embodied risk-taking, courage, sacrifice, openness to other cultures, and participation in life-changing work. That configuration makes an impression, even from afar.

It goes beyond these subjective impressions. Marie Balzer Wiebe, Anna Suderman Bergthold, and Esther Friesen Kroeker are among the relatively few historically significant people in my family tree.[5] In many positive ways and across multiple generations, they changed the communities in which they lived and worked, Marie's in the United States, Anna's in India, and Esther's in Mali.

*****

Sharon's brother, Paul, used to say that he had only two choices for his life's work: operate the family lumber business or become a Mennonite Brethren pastor. I assume he felt some obligation to continue the family tradition of working with wood and the Klassen family had a strong connection to the Mountain Lake lumber yard since at least 1920.

Yet for Paul's parents, church work (being a pastor or a missionary) trumped family tradition.

Soon after college, for reasons of his own, Paul decided that being a pastor would be his occupation. He probably wouldn't accept my use of the word "occupation" to describe what he does. Church ministry is his "vocation" or "calling." Both words suggest a religious or spiritual aspect in the choice of how one makes a living and, as noted at the start of this chapter, it is an activity where our joy and the needs of the world intersect.

During his nearly 40 years of ministry, Paul has pastored congregations in South Dakota and Oklahoma. In early March 2003, during a visit to Paul and Gladys' home in Edmond, Oklahoma,[6] Sharon and I attended a worship service in the local Mennonite Brethren church where Paul preached. It was the first Sunday after the United States military had invaded Iraq. Paul's sermon that Sunday gave us a glimpse of the challenges and calling of a pastor.

Paul's took his text from *The Gospel According to Luke* and told the story of two men at the temple praying. One expressed gratitude to God that he was not like other people: thieves, rogues, adulterers, or tax collectors. The other man, a tax collector, beat his breast and simply said, "God, be merciful to me, a sinner."[7]

God did not hear the first man's prayer, Paul said. But God heard the second man's prayer, forgave and restored him.

And then, toward the end of his sermon, Paul referred to the invasion of Iraq. God does not hear our prayers for victory, Paul said. He hears us when we confess our sins, including our desires for victory and our desires for control.

In Oklahoma, nearly everyone is strongly pro-military. Members of that congregation had served in the armed forces. And on that Sunday, after hundreds of thousands of soldiers had entered the battle, the prayers of a nation were with them. Yet Paul preached the text before him and courageously applied it to the leading issue of the day. I can't imagine it was a popular sermon. It was, however, the only anti-war message that congregation would have listened to on such an occasion.

*****

Among my brothers and me, teaching served as a bridge between the farm and something else. LeRoy taught high school students in Reedley, California after graduating from seminary and before pursuing a doctorate in ethics. Marley taught fourteen years in Kansas and

Minnesota before accepting the opportunity to buy into the Klassen family business. I taught two years in Iowa after completing my service with Mennonite Central Committee and before enrolling in law school.

For me, the entry into teaching was entirely pragmatic. I married at a young age and needed a steady income to support a married lifestyle. I enjoyed school and had been a good student, so teaching seemed a logical and achievable option.

It was more than that for Marley. He loved the creative and unpredictable space within a classroom where words and images spark a student's interest, emotion, and understanding. To get to that space, he spent hours mining pop culture for ideas and stage-setters. Music and photos were among his favorite tools.

Our father had served on the school board for Mountain Lake Public Schools during my high school years. It made for some embarrassing moments, such as when I brought home J.D. Salinger's *Catcher in the Rye.* The text angered Dad, who confronted the school librarian for having such trash on the school's shelves. But his school board service clearly communicated the value he placed on education, even though he had stopped attending after eighth grade.

Marley carried on that value in the family. Within a year of his return to Mountain Lake, he ran for and was elected to the school board. In 1983 and 1984 he chaired the board, and in 1985 ran for and won a second term. For him, education wasn't just a way to earn a living; it was a vocation.

Paycheck Living

After returning to Minnesota from Jamaica in July 1973, I tried but failed to get a teaching job. So we moved to Plan B. Sharon finished her under-graduate degree at St. Cloud State University in the spring of 1974, majoring in English with a library science minor. I pumped gas and got a job as a hallway monitor (bouncer) in a local junior high school.

During the spring Sharon graduated, I landed a job teaching American history, government, and economics to high school students in Pocahontas, Iowa. Sharon found work as a children's librarian and later as a bank teller. It was a culturally conservative town and most of the young women Sharon's age were having children. We wanted to start our family too, but Sharon didn't get pregnant until midway through my second year of teaching there. By then I had been accepted in law school. We decided to stay the course and moved to Minneapolis in

August, 1976. I began classes in September and Sharon gave birth to Amber soon after.

We lived in student housing. We weren't the only parents living there, but most women Sharon got to know were pursuing graduate degrees. And of course, the women I was getting to know in my classes were doing the same. So Sharon's experience went from small town Iowa without children to the university environment with a baby. The experience of being out of synch continued.

We had little money and got by with the help of student loans. To avoid borrowing any more than we had to, Sharon also worked as a secretary in the Office of Continuing Education for Women on the campus. As the name of the program suggests, it promoted opportunities for women at all stages of life to take classes and earn their degrees.

It was a wonderful place for Sharon to work, especially given the issues she felt during those years. In student housing and around the campus she tended to focus on the twenty-something women preparing for careers. Yet within her job, Sharon met women of all ages working to integrate child-bearing, family and career in a variety of ways. Some had their children early, some had them late, some didn't have children. There were trade-offs, to be sure, but women figured it out.

Over the next twenty years, balancing family and work became a major theme of Sharon's life.

Emily arrived at the end of 1978. Six months later, Sharon was back at work half-time, fretting about the adequacy of child care arrangements, but convinced she was a better mom if she had some time away from the girls. We needed her earnings, even after I got my law degree and passed the bar exam, because I accepted a job with a legal aid firm that did not pay enough to support the family without income from Sharon.

In late 1979, Fred Kopplin, a friend with a solo law practice, asked Sharon to work for him three days a week. Sharon accepted and thus began her connection to the law, first as a legal secretary and then as a paralegal. A solo law practice is a small business and Sharon was involved in many aspects of it. She enjoyed the work and felt invested in the firm's success, making friendships that have endured to this day.

In Lancaster, Sharon first followed the pattern she had established back in Minneapolis: work three days a week as a real estate and probate paralegal. Her tenure with Russell, Krafft and Gruber now exceeds twenty years. It's a medium-sized practice that treats its employees well and is less stratified than most law offices. Sharon knows she is valued and appreciated; she enjoys her colleagues, the variety in her work, and the relative independence with which she is able to function.

After Amber graduated high school and enrolled in college, Sharon began to work full-time. That continued until Emily and her husband, Guy, had their first child, Anna, in 2005.[8] Then Sharon reduced her work schedule to four days so she could provide care for Anna one day a week.

So Sharon has had a career, now exceeding thirty years in length. It began inauspiciously with an offer of employment from a friend. But it has evolved into what she had hoped it would be: challenging work in flexible environments with people she enjoys.

Back at the beginning, when Amber was three and Emily nearly one, it was only a part-time job as a secretary. It certainly didn't feel like a career. That generated feelings of shame and failure, especially during a decade such as the 1980s when progressive women were expected to be purposeful and assertive in reaching for the brass ring.

But family concerns have been paramount in Sharon's decision-making. Those concerns didn't always point in the same direction; the family needed her earnings, for example, and the children needed her attention and physical presence. So it has been a balancing act. She's been good at it.

From her point of view, nurturing the family is part of making a living. The family provides a place to eat, sleep, love, play, grow and change. If the family is getting along, it restores and empowers its members, enabling them to meet the challenges of the work-a-day world with perseverance and creativity. Most of us know we don't do well in our work when our family life is in disarray.

Beyond wrestling with the question of a career, Sharon also has confronted me at times about giving my work too much of my time and energy. I have justified myself by pointing to the moral urgency of the kind of work I've done. Sharon hasn't been persuaded by this, although she has granted me a measure of grace.

Part of our difficulty in this regard is attributable to our families of origin. I was raised in a family with defined gender roles. The concern for equity between husband and wife was understood as a matter of effort and contribution: is each spouse working hard? Is each contributing something important to the joint task of making a living? Dad was always busy. And no one ever suggested he wasn't holding up his end, even though he rarely did any work inside the house.

Sharon's perspective differed from mine in two ways. First, from her mother she understood equity to involve the sharing of work. Sharon hasn't agreed with my way of creating separate categories within the larger task of making a living. Second, she has observed we aren't living on a farm where I do the outside work and she the inside work. We both have jobs and there are no cows to milk or chickens to feed. Yet there are meals to be cooked, clothes to be washed, and a house to be cleaned.

Yes, Sharon has the stronger case. Still, the argument goes on!

*****

In this fast-paced era, we are told to expect many changes in places of employment and the kinds of work we do. Indeed, that's been the case for me. Still, my work life reflects other factors too, some personality-related and others related to the environment in which I was raised.

On a farm, work is a routine and unquestioned part of each day. That's unappealing, to be sure. But it is offset by the fact that one gets to do a variety of things. Some are terribly boring but they don't last long; tomorrow, there will be something else and the farmer has some measure of choice in what it will be. Success depends on being able to do a variety of things adequately. Not perfectly, but adequately.

Between growing up in that milieu and having a father with a restless and energetic spirit, I acquired a low tolerance for boredom. I have never wanted to make my living with work that disinterests me. This strikes me today as self-indulgent. Work is tedious at times for all of us and boredom a part of holding a job. Can a mature and responsible adult really insist on interesting work?

Well, I have insisted, perhaps to a fault. During my two years of teaching at Pochahontas High School, I noticed how bored the older teachers were, how tired they seemed of what they did to make a living. So even though I enjoyed teaching, I started plotting my escape, before we had children and I could no longer afford to leave.

Years later, when I was practicing law, a supervisor addressed this aspect of my personality by suggesting I was a dilettante: a person without strong professional commitment and only a superficial interest in a field of knowledge. That I still remember his comment shows he touched a nerve.

A second factor that shaped my approach to making a living was the Christian idealism with which I was raised. It taught me that through the power of God's abiding presence and blessing, I was a person the world wanted and needed. The point wasn't to build a career or some virtual edifice to myself but to make the world a better place.

For me, that meant getting involved in righting the imbalance between the powerful and the powerless. I never have held the view that the powerful are bad people and the powerless good. Instead, after our experience of living in Jamaica, I have thought of society in structural terms. Some people are valued and the benefits of society tend to flow toward them; others are devalued and they make do with the scraps. This dynamic, while prevalent in all times and places, drives the world toward ever-greater injustice unless people of goodwill join with the powerless to address the imbalance. It has always been obvious to me that I wanted to be part of the rebalancing.

This came into very narrow focus during the spring of my second year in law school. I was clerking for a private firm in Columbia Heights and doing fine. Everyone assumed I would work with that firm full-time over the summer. But then I became aware of an opportunity to work at the St. Paul American Indian Center, a storefront community agency on Payne Avenue with a tiny cubicle at the back staffed by a legal services attorney, Jan Werness. My choice of the Indian Center that summer opened doors to a two-year fellowship to represent native clients, eight additional years of practice with legal services in St. Paul, and the work I've done since. It was a fork in the road that changed my life's path.

There are many honorable ways to make a living. Human need, as expressed in this wonderfully complex experience called life, calls for great variety in the work we do. Within the vast array of possibilities, I have been drawn to work related to justice, to making the crooked places straight. Of course, defining injustice in a particular situation usually involves a struggle among competing perspectives. Throughout my life, I have felt energized by the opportunity to participate in that struggle. It hasn't been clear to me whether this energy grows from a healthy or unhealthy root, from a love for justice or conflict. Perhaps it was planted by Dad's participation in school-related controversies during my youth. However it got there, it has fueled my involvements over the years.

My work with legal services touched on many of the legal difficulties that precipitate crises in the lives of low-income individuals and their families. Evictions, utility shut-offs, marriage break-ups, job terminations, and the cut-off of public supports (food stamps, medical assistance) were all part of it.

From a career perspective, I achieved my greatest accomplishment at age 34. The law firm I worked for (Southern Minnesota Regional Legal Services) litigated on behalf of Hmong refugees, some of whom had collaborated with U.S. military forces during the war in Vietnam in the 1960s and 1970s. After the U.S. evacuation, the Hmong fled across the Mekong River into Laos. Some came to Minnesota during the early 1980s with the promise of 36 months of financial support and health care. Soon after taking office, President Reagan slashed their eligibility to eighteen months.

We sued the State of Minnesota in the summer of 1982, alleging that before cutting off these Hmong families, the State was required to give notice and an opportunity for the Hmong to demonstrate their eligibility for financial support and health care under other programs offered through the welfare system. Federal Judge Edward Devitt said no, the Hmong had been aware of such opportunities through the informal communications "grapevine". We appealed and the U.S. Eighth Circuit U.S. Court of Appeals reversed Judge Devitt.[9] Around 1,000 Hmong families secured continued financial and medical support because of that decision.

In 1985, the firm began a Farm Law Project to provide legal assistance to insolvent farmers facing foreclosure and liquidation of their property. Much of our work focused on educating farmers regarding their legal rights and mediating with lenders. I headed up the Project during its first two-plus years.

I am proud of my work with legal services and admire the people there with whom I worked. They saw entrenched injustice up close and yet remained committed to something better, earning far less than they could have in conventional law offices while facing long odds in the courtroom. Those who mentored me there, some as people of faith and others who were not, remain in my memory as role models and guides.

But litigation is not much valued within Mennonite circles, and I carried a sense that this way of making a living was not in synch with the tradition from which I came. That didn't keep me awake at night, but it may have contributed to my decision to join Mennonite Central Committee (MCC) as director of its U.S. Service Program.

MCC is about eliciting and sometime catalyzing the power of local communities to serve their own interests. It is less about government and more about the power of culture and people working within their own norms to makes their communities better. Perhaps because of the closer fit between MCC's mission and my background, it was my favorite place to make a living. It brought together my faith, my tradition, and the energy I feel when working at issues related to justice.

The MCC Service Program placed two-year volunteers in ministries and agencies working in distressed communities in south Florida, Atlanta, New Orleans, Washington, D.C., rural Kentucky, and rural South Dakota. It also placed volunteers in Lancaster County to serve MCC's administrative needs. In each location, we attempted to have a small group of volunteers who would provide mutual aid and spiritual support for one another and discern where they sensed God's spirit to be at work, asking how they could be part of strengthening the community's response. The core of my work consisted of working with the leadership of each local unit. I visited them twice a year and consulted frequently.

During my time with the Service Program, MCC began working in Pine Ridge, South Dakota. We also developed a congregation-based service option for adults who wanted to serve their own communities. This was designed for African American, Native and Hispanic youth, some of whom wanted to serve with MCC but were unwilling to leave their home communities, which needed them.

In 1993 I moved to the MCC executive office and began working with MCC's leader, John Lapp. My position focused on internal operations and fundraising and took me away from justice-related work. Yet within the MCC environment, many so-called administrative matters are reframed as issues of justice and so there remained plenty of opportunities to approach conflict with creativity and hope. Sometimes I did and sometimes I didn't; I write more about this in Chapter 4.

John retired in 1996 and Ron Mathies replaced him as MCC's leader. Ron was ambivalent about my staying on, so I decided to leave at the end of 1997. I accelerated my departure by a few months when I came out on the short end of a bureaucratic tug-a-war over moving staff positions from Pennsylvania to Manitoba.

That left me unemployed with two daughters in college. It was the scariest three months of my life. I applied for lots of jobs and interviewed lots of places. My principled concerns about vocation slowly melted away as the bank balance declined.

Then late one November afternoon, I received a phone call from Joni Rabinowitz, a Pittsburgh activist and president of the board at the Pennsylvania Hunger Action Center, inviting me to become its executive director. The invitation was a God-send and my stint with Hunger Action became my longest, lasting a bit over ten years.

Hunger Action focused on advocacy to state government in support of public policies to improve nutrition and reduce food insecurity. Our small staff (we never totaled more than seven) worked closely with the food banks and food pantries but did not distribute food. Instead, we staffed a statewide anti-hunger hotline that provided specific referrals for individuals and families in need of food assistance. We worked with local providers to strengthen what we called the food security safety net. We expanded nutrition education at food pantries, in schools, and at other venues. We promoted fresh fruit and vegetables at pantries, senior centers, schools, and through the federal supplemental food programs (WIC and Food Stamps). And we organized food pantry staff and recipients in support of an increase in the minimum wage. I was recognized for these activities by the Pennsylvania Department of Agriculture at its annual Farm Show dinner in January 2008.

Over the years, I worked most on improving the Food Stamp Program (now called SNAP). We helped people enroll but most of our work was policy-oriented advocacy. This involved frequent contact with Pennsylvania state agency personnel and with staff in congressional offices, especially during the effort every five or six years to reauthorize the Farm Bill, which includes SNAP and WIC. Hunger Action played a significant role in expanding access by working families to this program. In 2005, at its national advocacy conference, the Food Research and Action Center named me the first recipient of its Raymond Wheeler/Paul Wellstone Anti-Hunger Leadership Award.

I "retired" from the Hunger Action Center in early 2008, having run out of ideas for moving the Center forward and convinced someone else would be more successful at fundraising. I moved directly to a position with a new coalition that had come together, the Pennsylvania Health Access Network. It hired me as public affairs manager, which meant I was responsible for media relations, government relations, and some aspects of mobilizing the public in support of health care reform.

The coalition came together in an attempt to pass state legislation to expand health insurance coverage through a creative combination of state and federal funding, much like the approach Massachusetts had modeled a few years earlier. Governor Ed Rendell was solidly behind the plan and made it a key objective for his second term. Our job was to let the public know about this opportunity and organize their support into effective citizen advocacy. During the 2008 legislative session we nearly got it done, only to have our efforts thwarted by a combination of Republican opposition in the state senate and the economic collapse on Wall Street in September of that year.

It was ground-breaking work and I felt lucky to be involved. Yet it also turned out to be the roughest job I've had. The members of the coalition – labor unions, faith-based groups, nonprofit agencies, health educators, advocates for seniors -- shared the same goals but not the same methods and lacked a history of working in a coordinated fashion. My job, in part, was to bridge those divides, nurture more collaboration, and build an effective coalition. Early on, it became clear that the labor side of the coalition was dissatisfied with my work.

In the spring of 2009, after the inauguration of Barack Obama as U.S. president, the Coalition pivoted from state-based advocacy to community organizing in support of national reform. The labor organizations in the Coalition went into full campaign mode and expected other coalition members to follow their lead. But campaign mode is not the same thing for nonprofit groups as it is for a labor union. So the fissures in the Coalition widened and I had little success in changing that. In November, just before the first crucial vote in the United States House of Representatives, the Coalition eliminated my position and laid me off. I found myself living the words of bluesman Greg Brown, "No matter how we plan and rehearse, we're at pink slip's mercy in a paper universe."[10]

As I'm writing these paragraphs, I'm sixty-one years old and in an unenviable spot. That is, despite plenty of education, lots of diligent effort, and successful stints in difficult jobs, I don't have an established career and I am again looking for work. This suggests I've taken a wrong turn somewhere along the way. Yet I don't regret the path I've taken. My skills and aptitudes have been well-used and in ways that connected me to a larger purpose. And I've been blessed with colleagues I enjoyed and respected. Taken together, that has made for a pleasing vocation.

Looking back, the one aspect I feel most uneasy about is how little time I've committed to friendship and simple neighborliness. I was always too busy. The following poem reflects some of this; I wrote it while working at Hunger Action.

This is the Day

I should know better by now
how to live day by day
grateful, expectant, open-hearted,
encountering God along the way.

Instead I mold time into bunches
each one named by my desire
seeking out a grand commission
to hold my interest ‘til I tire.

Once death tried to take me captive;
no more tomorrows, it seemed to say.
Yet, perversely, I resist contentment
reaching instead for quixotic dreams.

And so I am left, still learning
to pay attention to things close by;
not to look past this day’s treasure
while squinting at the distant sky.

Tomorrow morning when I awaken
the day’s blank slate in my mind’s eye
I’ll yearn again for buoyant mission
to bear me up through doubts and sighs.

Or maybe birdsong will catch my ear
I’ll feel love’s hand upon my skin;
maybe things too small to mention
will enlarge my living, fill me in.

The Formative Power of Work

Generally, we pay the most attention to the dramatic and unusual events of life: exotic travel, a great adventure, a tragic occurrence, a noteworthy achievement. Yet those moments do not define us; instead, we are shaped by the constancy and repetition of what we do nearly every day. Making a living is something we do nearly every day; that’s why it is such a powerful force in our lives.

During the 1990s, historian Christopher Lasch shaped my thinking about making a living and its connections with the broader political reality. I read his *True and Only Heaven – Progress and Its Critics* early in the decade, at a time when I was working at Mennonite Central Committee and needed an understanding of American society that better integrated my experiences as a legal service attorney, father of two teen-age daughters, and director of a volunteer placement program meant to support community development.

Lasch wrote out of his "sense of foreboding" for a society increasingly controlled by huge and implacable business corporations and the military. These powers, he wrote, "operate without regard to any rational objectives except their own self-aggrandizement."[11] His critique began to take shape during the Vietnam War, when he concluded that "not merely [did] our public officials no longer care about the truth but they had lost even the capacity to distinguish it from falsehood." As for the media, "disinformation monopolized the airwaves."

I was familiar with this sort of critique, generally offered by authors with a left-wing perspective. But Lasch had far more to say. He wrote of "the unexpectedly rigorous business of bringing up children" and about the "icy indifference" in American society "to everything that makes it possible for children to flourish and to grow up to be responsible adults." And he wrote: "To see the modern world from the point of view of a parent is to see it in the worst possible light. This perspective unmistakably reveals the unwholesomeness . . . . of our way of life."

Lasch's bill of particulars included our obsession with sex and violence, our addiction to drugs and to entertainment, our impatience with the constraints of marital and familial ties, our reluctance to draw a distinction between right and wrong, our overgrown military, our hostility to immigrants, and the widely held assumption that only those children born for success ought to be allowed to be born at all.

And then he addressed what he considered the heart of the matter.

> "At every level of American society, it [is] becoming harder for people to find work that self-respecting men and women [can] throw themselves into with enthusiasm. The degradation of work represent[s] the most fundamental sense in which institutions no longer command public confidence. It [is] the most important source of the 'crisis of authority' so widely deplored but so little understood. The authority conferred by a

calling, with all its moral and spiritual overtones, [can] hardly flourish in a society in which the practice of a calling [has] given way to a particularly vicious kind of careerism."[12]

How do we become a society where the financial and military sectors do not dominate and Hollywood and consumerism do not hollow us out? Lasch asserted that would require a reassessment of work. Much of his 500 page book described the debate during the 19th century when such questions were front and center. It pitted liberals who embraced industrial capitalism as the path to prosperity against populists who wanted a future in which most people worked as producers and thereby developed the traits required by a free society.

By the end of the 19th century, those who perceived themselves to be progressive and forward-thinking had triumphed over the populists. As a result, the corporation became the object of special protection under the law and those who controlled capital and credit became dominant in our economic life. Many Americans held jobs they hated but could not afford to leave, their greatest aspiration being an annual raise that would enable them to consume more cheaply-produced goods. The number of artisans, tradesmen, and small farmers dwindled. These dynamics accelerated throughout the 20th century, culminating during the 1990s with passage of the North America Free Trade Agreement (NAFTA).

Before reading Lasch, it had not occurred to me that a "nation of hirelings" lacks the capacity to be anything but passive, and that for a society to remain free, it needs a broad base of independent producers. It had not occurred to me that most of the energy for economic justice in America had been supplied by the artisan class, not laborers working for a wage. It had not occurred to me that America once had a strong public movement opposed to industrial capitalism and supportive of traditional community values. I felt like I had been born a century too late![13]

Of course, Lasch so affected me for personal reasons. He described the connection between the kind of people Sharon and I came from – small farmers and merchants, artisans and craftsmen – and the larger cause of justice to which I felt committed. He reminded me that what we do every day to make a living shapes us. To be the courageous, ethical and independently-minded people we admire, we need to pay attention to how we make a living. It involves more than a paycheck.

*****

Having been a "wage-slave"[14] all my life, I naturally attempt to deal with my current unemployment by searching for an employer who will hire me. Even while I continue such efforts, I find myself reflecting on how our ancestors made a living without paychecks. They relied on skills and ingenuity to fill niches their communities found valuable. Perhaps that is the model I need to recover for myself during our pre-retirement years; perhaps it is the model many of us will need to recover in a world increasingly characterized by economic dislocation.

Certainly there are signs that the astonishing U.S. prosperity during the latter half of the 20th century was an aberration. Our country emerged from World War II as one of very few with a functioning industrial economy and an educated workforce. The world was eager for U.S. products, raw materials were cheap and the U.S. dollar was the world's currency. In domestic politics, a consensus supported strategies to build the middle class through the sharing of wealth and opportunity. Together, these factors created an economic climate that fueled growth and rising standards of living.

None of those critical factors remains in place. This suggests future generations will live closer to the economic edge than our generation has. Meeting that challenge will require adaptations not unlike those our ancestors made. Two of their strongest assets, trust in God's abiding care and membership in a practical community of support, are likely to take on new relevance as the American dream continues to fade.

I wrote the following poem while reflecting on vocation and the challenges of job transitions as one grows older. At the time, Sharon and I were at the Still Waters retreat near Carlisle, Pennsylvania. It includes a lovely guest cottage made entirely of recycled materials.

Fitted

My eye is drawn to the beams,
scarred and bowed, notched and fitted,
squaring the cottage and holding it erect.
I am in the company of the old,
the irregular, the full-dimensioned.
Reclaimed and efficacious
in a rough-hewn way.

"Age is a state of mind," they say
to us who are sagging a bit
after years of heavy lifting.
True enough, yet I can't help but notice
they're looking past me
for a standard fit,
not what I have to offer.

I have no argument with them;
they've assessed me accurately enough.
And just ahead a place awaits
where I will be joined and fitted;
a room to help square,
a load to help support
in my irregularity.

---

[1] Buechner, Frederick. *Wishful Thinking: A Theological ABC,* Harper and Row, 1973 at 95.

[2] Driedger, Johannes. "Farming Among Mennonites in West Prussia and East Prussia." *Global Anabaptist Mennonite Encyclopedia Online,* 1956

[3] *80th Anniversary Booklet 1877-1957,* published by the Carson and Mountain Lake Mennonite Brethren churches, 1957 at 26.

[4] Wiebe, Katie Funk and Richard D. Thiessen. "Bergthold, Anna G. Suderman (1875-1957)." *Global Anabaptist Mennonite Encyclopedia*

Online. January 2006. A small part of Anna's story is included in Viola Bergthold Wiebe's *Sepia Prints*, Kindred Press, 1990.

[5] Also in that group of notables are Abraham W. Friesen and grandsons Abraham L. Friesen, Abraham F. Thiessen and Johann P. Thiessen.

[6] Paul and Gladys' children are Miriam, Rebecca, and Stephen.

[7] *The Gospel According to Luke*, Chapter 18, verses 9-14.

[8] Emily and Guy's second child, Elena, was born in September, 2008.

[9] Chu Drua Cha vs. Noot, 696 F2d 594 (U.S. 8th Circuit Court of Appeals, 1982).

[10] Brown, Greg. "Just a Bum" from *In the Dark With You,* Red House Records, 1985.

[11] Lasch, Christopher. *The True and Only Heaven: Progress and Its Critics,* W.W. Norton & Company, 1991 at 33.

[12] Id.

[13] The 20th Century had its own proponents of an economy built around production rather consumption In addition to Lasch, Dorothy Day of the Catholic Worker movement and Wendell Berry often wrote about this.

[14] The term "wage slave" comes out of 19th century rhetoric and was meant to decry the development of industrial capitalism and the erosion of respect for those who contribute their labor to the production of goods and services.

"Tis all in peeces, all coherence gone;
all just supply, and all relations:
Prince, Subject, Father, Sonne, are all things forgot,
for every man alone thinkes he hath got
to be a Phoenix, and that then can bee
none of that kinde, of which he is, but hee."[1]
John Donne

"What we find hard to see
is that it is the extreme fragmentation of the modern world
that really threatens our individuation;
that what is best in our separation and individuation,
our sense of dignity and autonomy as persons,
requires a new integration if it is to be sustained."[2]
Robert Bellah

Chapter 3: With whom will we join?

Mostly, we join groups that make no claims about how the world should be managed. Card-playing clubs, book groups, and birding enthusiasts are examples. But other acts of joining bring us into alignment with one or another point of view about broader society. It is such acts that this chapter is about.

The reader is likely to wonder if the stories in this chapter will provide any support for our modern tendency to avoid groups that presume to provide a big-picture view of life and the world.

As best I can tell, our ancestors did not perceive that to be an option. Apparently, they understood their capacity to flourish as individuals to require membership in a group that would help them find their way through life in a way that honored the truth about life. For them, it was always about which group to join, not whether to go it alone.

Political Groups

On Labor Day 1969, Dad raised an American flag at his and Mom's farm. The entry in Mom's diary is succinct: "Dad cemented in a tall flag pole beside our chimney and pulled the flag up on it. It's real nice."

Mennonites generally don't fly the flag and I don't recall ever seeing a flag at our home growing up. In vain I have looked through Mom's diary for an explanation. Apparently, she thought such was unnecessary, although I recall conversation with my brothers about it. We wondered if it had something to do with us and Dad's unhappiness with our more leftwing political views.

Sharon and I had married only a few weeks before. Marriage was an act of emancipation for me, meaning I was no longer a member of Dad and Mom's household. Perhaps that's why I never engaged Dad in conversation about his flag.

How did Dad come to this decision? Was he following someone else's example? I have no answers to such questions. What seemed obvious to me at the time was that he wanted to associate himself with some message the flag represented, such as patriotism and love of country. Those were the days of street protests against the Vietnam War. It was the first year of the Nixon Administration, a time when at least thirty American soldiers died each day in a war President Johnson and his advisors had decided was a lost cause but then expanded anyway.

By associating himself with a patriotic message, I think Dad was attempting to join a broader political movement in America reasserting traditional values. Street protesters, from this perspective, were part of the problem, not part of the solution. Had I read an author like Christopher Lasch in those days, I might have better understood and even empathized with Dad. As it was, I perceived him to want to reestablish authority, no matter what the cost in terms of justice. I saw him moving in a reactionary direction.

By raising the flag, was Dad also communicating his rejection of the traditional Mennonite ambivalence toward national governments? Mennonites have long recognized a God-given role for government to maintain order and punish criminals. But because national governments typically overreach, claiming a degree of allegiance that Mennonites believe belongs only to God, Mennonites have been careful to keep their emotional distance. Dad seemed to be narrowing that distance.

Thirty-five years later, I did some narrowing of my own as I became active for the first time in a political campaign to elect a president of the United States. With the U.S. invasion of Iraq and threats of more military action against other nations, I felt I could no longer remain aloof from the partisan political process. And so I used vacation days to volunteer with the local John Kerry campaign, going door-to-door in neighborhoods of suburban Lancaster to engage people in conversations about why it was important to send George Bush packing.

What strikes me in retrospect is a similarity between Dad raising the flag and my campaigning to elect John Kerry as the next commander-in-chief of the world's dominant military. Each of us in our different ways was elevating the American state in our understandings of what was important for us to do. Because we acted out of Christian motivation, perhaps one could even say we each took a small step toward identifying God's work in the world with the health and well-being of the American state. [3]

*****

Political controversy clouded my enrollment in Delft school as a first-grader. District 16 had no high school; it provided instruction only for grades 1-8. Students who wanted grades 9-12 attended Mountain Lake High School under a special arrangement. This apparently was unsatisfactory to Mountain Lake School District officials, who wanted the tiny Delft district to disband and become part of the larger Mountain Lake district.

In August of 1954, the people of Delft voted resoundingly to keep control of their own school. The Mountain Lake School District responded by announcing it would no longer accept Delft high school students. So on the day after Labor Day, Marley and I boarded a school bus driven by Uncle Pete and went to school in Delft, he in seventh grade and I in first. LeRoy stayed home and helped Dad with the farm work. He had no school to attend.

Dad and Mom were agitated by all of this, as were our neighbors. Controversy swirled through the community. At some point, a consensus emerged in support of consolidation because Delft simply could not maintain a high school for its few students. Then the question shifted: should the consolidation be with the Mountain Lake School District, which had precipitated this trouble, or with the Windom School District, which was larger and better equipped?

As LeRoy remembers that time, Dad viewed Mountain Lake as the better choice. Its student body was about fifty percent Mennonite and its leadership long accustomed to churchly concerns related to the content and scheduling of extracurricular activities. In Dad's view, that was preferable to the Windom district, where his sons would rub shoulders primarily with students from Lutheran and Roman Catholic families.

Other neighbors favored Windom and the community began to take sides. Tensions rose. Dad became a partisan in this conflict by joining a few others in circulating a petition in support of Mountain Lake. A "brother" in the church called Dad "a communist." Relatives and friends privately supported Dad's efforts but fell silent when others were present.

Several evenings during September, people gathered at the school house in Delft to debate and organize for action. It also happened to be campaign season (Val Bjornson vs. Hubert Humphrey for U.S. Senate), and in my memories the contention around the future of my school merge with my first awareness that people held different views about who to choose as our political leaders. "Dead rats, pickled cats, good enough for the Democrats!" was the phrase we children chanted to each other on the playground as we waited for those school consolidation meetings to end.

It was a memorable time for me because people in my parents' social circle (church members and neighbors) didn't talk much about politics. Most everyone had Republican sympathies and liked President Eisenhower, the Kansas son of an Anabaptist mother. One family in our congregation, led by David and Minnie Ewert, appeared to be an outlier; they appreciated Hubert Humphrey and displayed a Farmers Union sign at the end of their driveway. But generally, even in conversations with the Ewerts, electoral politics didn't get much attention.

In late September, the school crisis was over. Mom wrote:

> "Our district 16 has been dissolved and [the] county commissioners have put us into Mt. Lake District. So finally the thing is settled, though not to everybody's satisfaction."

This controversy, small as it was in the larger scope of things, made a big impression on me. It was my first encounter with community politics. I saw how Dad paid a price for his involvement in strained relationships with friends and neighbors who disagreed with the position he took. And I admired him for speaking up.

Two years later, our family relived one facet of this story when the Mennonite evangelist, George Brunk, came to Mountain Lake to host two weeks of revival meetings. He erected a huge tent for the occasion, laid a saw-dust trail down the center, and filled the rest of the space with folding chairs. Mom and Dad attended each meeting, usually with us boys in tow. Driving home one night from the tent site, the atmosphere in the car seemed charged with emotion. I couldn't fathom it and asked Mom what was wrong. She assured me nothing was wrong, only that Dad had been moved by the preacher's message to seek reconciliation with a neighbor from whom he had been estranged since the school consolidation controversy two years earlier. My brothers and I were awe-struck at this news. To our way of thinking, our father had done something wrong, something that would not go away, but had re-emerged at the tent meeting under the Holy Spirit's convicting power. And he had gone to the neighbor to make peace.

Still, we gathered from what Mom said that the neighbor had been less than gracious in accepting Dad's apology. As far we were concerned, that clinched it; Dad had been in the right all along.

*****

Over fifty years later, one of the adult Sunday school classes at our congregation in Lancaster spent a dozen Sundays talking about politics. We invited guests to speak to us: a Mennonite state legislator; a Mennonite lawyer who represented Pennsylvania's leading pro-life group; a Mennonite businessman who followed politics but did not vote and stayed away from all political associations; and a Mennonite organizer who supported progressive causes at the national level.[4] We reviewed the historic Mennonite aloofness from political activity.

And we asked the question: are we spending too much of our volunteer time in church and not enough in politics? After all, God in Christ is making all things new. Don't we betray that truth when we act like only church-related work is worthy of our volunteer time?

In the end, we fudged our answer. Yes, maybe we should get more involved in politics, but only a certain kind. We came up with four modest rules-of-thumb to describe the politics we thought deserving of more time and attention.

- It should focus on solutions to problems rather than partisan electoral results. Of course, labels (Democratic or Republican, liberal or conservative) will be attached to what we do; that can't be avoided. But that's not where our loyalties lie.

- It should articulate and embody positive alternatives for our society, such as alternative energy sources and lifestyles that would require less oil and a less aggressive foreign policy.

- It should be local, bringing us together with neighbors who may share our values and approaches to issues, even though they may not share our faith.

- It should be grounded in the teaching we receive in our congregation about the Kingdom of God, about the American empire in which we reside, and about the many points of tension between the two.

Civil Society in Poland and Prussia

Mennonites in Prussia and Poland steadfastly avoided the militancy the Dutch Anabaptists had shown in the 1530s. But life there was hardly without political conflict. Indeed, white-knuckled confrontations with authorities were a staple of the 250 years our ancestors lived there. While some historians see this period as a time when Mennonites became selfish and apolitical, that strikes me as a superficial reading. Public controversy was a consistent feature of their lives.

For Mennonites living in cities, the most immediate issues were citizenship and commercial relations with the guilds. To qualify for citizenship, one had to participate fully in a city's defense. The Mennonite refusal to take up arms and participate in local militias was usually an outright disqualification.

This had direct commercial implications because one could not join a guild if not a citizen. And if not a member of a guild, then one could not practice the trade to which the guild was committed. Thus, although Mennonite weavers introduced lace-making to Prussia in the late 1500s, the lace-making guild attempted to stop Mennonites from selling their own products.

This tense dynamic played itself out repeatedly as guilds sought to invoke the authority of city government to restrict the sales of Mennonite tradespeople. The guilds were an important constituency and city governments generally tried to meet their demands. But officials also loathed putting Mennonite craftsmen out of business, in part because their business activities brought money into city coffers.

In Danzig, these dynamics reached a crisis point during the years of 1749-1752. The guilds commenced a public relations campaign designed to turn the public against Mennonite-made products. The city council imposed special fees on Mennonite craftsmen. Up to quarter of the Mennonite families in Danzig left and moved to Koenigsberg or back to the Netherlands. Even the government of the Netherlands got involved via a memorandum to the Danzig city council expressing concern about the treatment of the Mennonites.

At other times, the Mennonites' religious beliefs became the flash point. During the 1600s, as the Counter-Reformation gathered momentum in Poland, Catholic leaders, often with the support of government officials, scrutinized the orthodoxy of Anabaptist theology. The Polish parliament debated whether to expel Mennonites along with the Unitarians. (The King, concerned about the potential loss of revenue from Mennonite farmers, intervened on their behalf.) A lengthy interrogation of two Mennonite pastors by the Catholic bishop occurred at a public hearing in Danzig in 1678.

In rural areas, the payment of church dues was a chronic source of tension. Mennonites often were required to pay dues to both the Catholic and Lutheran churches, especially as they moved from being lessees to being land owners. Mennonites were reconciled to the need to pay one or the other, but chafed at paying both, something no other religious group was required to do, and often raised this issue with the authorities.

From 1600 to 1720, Poland and Sweden fought several very destructive wars on the lands around the Vistula River. Farmers were expected to provide foodstuffs for whatever army occupied the area. This unofficial tax was a major burden for all farmers, including Mennonites.

The authorities in Danzig required Mennonites to pay for the extra soldiers hired to take the place of young Mennonites who refused to participate in the armed protection of the city. Eventually, the Mennonite position moderated a bit and its members served as firefighters during canon bombardments. When Frederick the Great gained control of the Delta in 1772, he mandated both civilian service during wartime and the payment of additional taxes in lieu of military service.

Frederick the Great was known to appreciate the Mennonites, especially their economic contributions. Because of this and despite his reputation as a military man, his control of the Delta region elicited cautious hope in Mennonite communities. When he first visited the

Delta and the town of Marienburg to celebrate Prussian acquisition of the new territory, Mennonites saw an opportunity to further strengthen the King's positive perception. They attended the event and presented him with a gift from the products of their farms: two oxen ready for his table, four hundred pounds of butter, twenty cakes of cheese, and an assortment of chickens and ducks. Their lobbying may be where the common phrase, "buttering him up" comes from.[5]

Along with the tasty gift, the Mennonites also conveyed a specific request: a petition requesting Frederick to confirm their traditional liberties, including exemption from military service. The king received both the food and the petition graciously and within a month issued a statement affirming his respect for religious liberty and the right of everyone to seek salvation in their own fashion. But the statement said nothing about the subject in the Mennonite petition, exemption from military service.

Meanwhile, the Prussian government commenced a census of people living in the area of the Delta. This alarmed Mennonites, who saw it as preparation for the conscription of young men into the military, and they protested to government officials. Again Frederick promptly responded to their concerns, but with a policy that raised new concerns: Mennonites were exempted from military service and could have their own churches and schools, but were forbidden to buy land from non-Mennonites except by special permission from the war ministry. In addition, the Mennonites were required to make an annual payment of 5,000 Thalers for the support of the military officers' academy at Culm. As stated by historian C. Henry Smith, "Frederick finally decided that money was as essential to a program of conquest as soldiers, and as hard to get."[6]

While some Mennonites were uneasy with this arrangement and its distinction between direct and indirect service, most were willing to accept it. Indeed, Mennonite payments for the support of the Culm military academy continued for nearly one hundred years.

Under Polish tradition and law, the right to own land was linked to the duty to participate in the sovereign's military. As we have seen, Mennonites were prepared to make payments in lieu of military service, but not to take up arms and serve. This became the central point of contention. The Prussian kings were soldier-kings, committed to a strong military and determined to build it through the participation of citizen-soldiers, not mercenaries. The Mennonites, on the other hand, were primarily a farming people and needed be expand their land holdings via purchases from neighbors.

And so negotiations continued. In 1777, Mennonite leaders again formally petitioned Frederick to relax restrictions on land purchases, to guarantee their right to pursue all occupations, to be relieved of paying dues to both the Catholic and Lutheran churches, and for relief from special military assessments. Again Frederick responded with a formal charter in 1780 exempting Mennonites from military service "forever", reiterating the liberty of all people to seek "salvation" in their own ways, and somewhat relaxing the restrictions on land purchases. He also approved nearly 300 pending Mennonite requests to purchase land that had not previously been in Mennonite hands.

But by 1786, with the death of "Ole Fritz," the era of compromise was over. His successor, Frederick Wilhelm III, issued the Edict for the Future Regulation of Mennonite Affairs in which he affirmed the Mennonites' historic right to practice their religion but went on to describe it as a personal matter, largely unrelated to public life. The Edict went on highlight the King's duty to "defend the fatherland" and provide for national security. To accomplish this, the Edict curtailed future purchases of land by Mennonites and rescinded recent purchases by Mennonites. As stated in an official report, the 400 farms that had passed into Mennonite hands between 1772 and 1782 "could produce a whole regiment" if young men on those farms were subject to military conscription. [7]

For Mennonite families with several sons, the Edict and the policies of the new king left little-to-no prospect of acquiring enough land to keep their sons engaged in farming.

The pressure on the Mennonites continued to build during the Napoleonic Wars of the early 1800s. Mennonite leaders attempted to support the Prussian government's effort by donating 30,000 Thalers in addition to the usual special levies and horses. The donation was accompanied by a request that the money be used to alleviate suffering caused by the war. But the Mennonites also made it clear that "we leave it to your Royal Majesty's gracious will to determine its disposition."

As the wars continued and Napoleon's forces pressed triumphantly on, the Mennonites made more payments – first 10,000 Thalers and then an additional 25,000 Thalers plus 500 horses. These payments were due on very short notice and many families were unable to meet their obligations as quickly as required. To avert a further crisis, wealthy families advanced the funds on behalf of the community.

Napoleon's forces inflicted a massive defeat on Prussian forces at Jena in 1806. Soon after, Napoleon's forces occupied all of southern Poland and moved north toward Danzig, Elbing and Koenigsberg. In response, Prussian authorities formed emergency local militias and summoned all able-bodied men to join. The Mennonites supplied yet more money and material and agreed to provide men to help with transportation and support services. But they refused to take up arms. This triggered intense criticism from Catholic and Lutheran neighbors who asked why Mennonites could claim special privileges when an enemy was invading the homeland. No amount of material support could take the place of sons killed or maimed in battle.

At the local level, many heated disputes occurred. On occasion, the authorities jailed fathers whose sons would not serve and seized sons whose eligibility for exemptions had been called into question.

Throughout this period, Mennonite delegations made repeated overtures to Prussian officials in an effort to secure confirmation of their traditional military exemption. Although these overtures always were well-received, the requested confirmation never came. In 1814, the Prussian government introduced universal military service; Mennonites were not mentioned, meaning they would be treated like everyone else. By then, however, many had already left Poland for what they hoped would be a less political and less complicated life in Russia.

Joining the Military

David von Riesen, a distant cousin at most, responded to the call to arms from the Prussian government. Although a member of the Elbing-Ellerwald Mennonite Church, he served in the Prussian army during the final stages of the Napoleonic wars and probably participated in the Battle of Waterloo.

Von Riesen's congregation promptly expelled him from membership because he had joined the military.

When he returned home from military service, von Riesen sought reinstatement into his home congregation or membership in the Danzig Mennonite Church. Neither would have him unless he repented of the sin of joining the military. Von Riesen then sued these congregations, an act he must have known would not cause them to become more welcoming. The case was negotiated at length but eventually went to judgment in Berlin, where his claims against the congregations were rejected.

According to historian Elizabeth H. Bender, the story of David von Riesen and the Mennonites was adapted for the stage and presented repeatedly in major German theater venues beginning in 1882 as *Der Menonit.* It portrayed the Mennonite people as unpatriotic. Mennonite church leaders objected; the play did not accurately describe their views or their conduct, they said. The author of the drama, Ernst von Wildenbruch, agreed that perhaps the script included some exaggeration but justified his script as poetic license necessary to render the moral message of the play. The play was last staged just prior to World War I.[8]

As should be obvious by now, opposition to military service has been a huge factor in our family history and played a leading role in the moves from Poland to Russia and from Russia to the United States. How has our family responded to conscription in the United States?

During World War I, conscription began in the United States before a system was in place for processing those individuals who opposed participation in war based on reasons of faith and conscience. This meant that Mennonite (and other) men were drafted and commenced military training before their status was clarified. U.S. military officials viewed this situation as ideal in that it provided the opportunity to persuade vulnerable inductees to comply with full military participation.

Some Mennonite men were persuaded, perhaps including a great-uncle, Peter Wiens. He served in the utilities detachment of the U.S. Army's Quarter Master Corps, a unit that generally did not engage in combat but was fully militarized by 1917. Others refused to train for anything but noncombatant roles within the military. Still others refused to put on the uniform and insisted on noncombatant service outside the military. This latter group of individuals, numbering around 1,300 Mennonites, experienced the most difficulty. A total of 138 were court-martialed and sent to prison; several Mennonite men died there due to the harsh conditions.

When the United States entered World War II, a system to process the claims of conscientious objectors was already in place, ready to be used prior to induction. Those with claims validated by local draft boards as genuine were sent to special Civilian Public Service (CPS) camps to do "work of national importance." About 12,000 draftees were processed in this way; 4,700 were Mennonites.

Among the Old Order Mennonite groups (the *Kleine Gemeinde,* for example), at least 90 percent of the men drafted served in CPS camps. But across all American Mennonite groups, only 46 percent of draftees served in that way; 14 percent served in noncombatant roles within the military and 40 percent served in the regular military units. Looking at CPS service within the two Mennonite groups with the largest presence in Minnesota, "the Mennonite Brethren [had] 36.4 percent and the General Conference Mennonite Church, 26.6 percent."[9] The majority of draftees from those two groups, in other words, served in either regular military or noncombatant military roles.

That was the case in my family. Uncles Jack, Arnie and Ed Wiens served as army combatants in Europe and Uncle Jack Friesen as an army noncombatant in the Pacific. LeRoy reflected on this part of our history.

> "Near the end of the time [my family lived] on the Redding farm, World War II came to an end. Three of my mother's brothers, and one of my father's, had served in the European theatre, and now they returned home. I was impressed by the jaunty angle of their caps and the aura of their uniforms. And I was fascinated without end with the rifles, shells and other memorabilia they [the three Wiens uncles] brought back and with which I secretly played in their upstairs closets. I remember sitting in the living room of my grandparents' home and clinging to every word these handsome soldiers said."

I wish my family had a different story to tell about its participation in World War II, one that had my uncles living in Civilian Public Service camps, jumping out of airplanes to fight fires or doing other "work of national importance."

But I also feel sympathy for my uncles and the choices they made. The cause as they knew it was just and many of their contemporaries responded with a willingness to sacrifice their lives. If no other cause of equal urgency and idealism called them to join (and I really don't know what kind of teaching their congregations provided during the '30s), then I can't blame them for responding to the call they received.

Yet it also must be acknowledged that my uncles' decisions to take up arms marked a watershed in our family's history. Our ancestors left Poland to prevent this from happening there, and then left Russia yet again for the same reason. Obviously, this history of sacrifice and commitment had lost its power.

Looking back to that time in his life, LeRoy does not recall any word or act from our parents to indicate the magnitude of what had happened, not even a private expression of personal opposition to military service for reasons of faith and conscience. My experience matches LeRoy's. Apparently, the shift wasn't only reflected in my somewhat wayward uncles; it had occurred lots of places, including my parents' home.

To be sure, the pendulum did not swing entirely to the other side. The pastors who taught Sharon and me during the '50s and early '60s[10] encouraged us to understand nonresistance as part of God's desire for our lives and as our response to God's love and mercy. When I appeared before the Cottonwood County Draft Board in the spring of 1970 to defend my claim to be a conscientiously opposed to participation in war, Dad supported me and also accompanied me to the hearing.

But as generations to come look back on our family's history on participation in war, they will see it is very mixed. It will be most accurate to say that some joined the military, some declined due to reasons of faith and conscience, and others managed to avoid dealing with the matter entirely.

In one sense, this divided house is not surprising because the entire Christian community is divided on this. Jesus told us to love our enemies, which means we won't kill them. That's the teaching most Mennonite and Quaker churches continue to emphasize. But Jesus also told us to love our neighbors, which means we will protect them from harm. That's the teaching the Lutherans, the Catholics, and the evangelicals continue to emphasize.

Our calling, if we believe Jesus is the one sent from God to save the world, is to embrace both teachings. We don't have the luxury of choosing one over the other.

The fact that this is extremely difficult does not mean we should despair of trying and let the government decide for us. This critical decision about the use of violence is at the very heart of the way of life Jesus invited us to join.[11] Why would we delegate such a matter to the government? Many public officials are well-intentioned and, within the scope of their authority, act in good faith. But even the best of them are not qualified to decide how we live out our commitments to Jesus. Yet this is what governments presume to be their prerogative regarding the use of violence.

First, they tell us who the enemy is through regular reports in our newspapers and the evening news. Some of those reports are based on the truth but much of it is propaganda, meant to dehumanize a rival and prepare us to lust for the deaths of its citizens.

Then the government defines the options for dealing with this enemy. Usually, it tells us all legitimate options have been pursued in seeking peace and that violence is the only remaining choice. Of course, our religious traditions also describe options for interacting with our enemies. But with our attention fixed on the evening news and scary things being said there, the teachings of our faith become oddly irrelevant as compared to the government's outline of "responsible actions" and "realistic options."

Finally, as part of joining the military, the government tells us who to kill and when to pull the trigger. These critical decisions, which we may agree can not be answered categorically for all times and places, are for those in the military delegated to their commanding officers.

This is wrong and it is why the Anabaptist refusal to join the military speaks so clearly to all Christians. You may not be a pacifist; I am not sure I am one either. Our personal purity is not the critical issue here. What is critical is Jesus' call to love our enemies as well as those who may be our enemies' victims. We will not learn to do both by joining the military. We will learn that only by joining a group whose discernment is rooted in honesty and truth and whose imagination and creativity are fired by some source other than government press releases.

Joining the Bar

Is it right for a Mennonite to practice law? Can one join the legal fraternity without jettisoning what the Anabaptists and Mennonites held dear? Those were the questions that filled my head in the spring of 1976 as I neared the end of my tenure as a high school social studies teacher.

Sharon and I had visited two of the law schools that had accepted me, the University of Iowa and the University of Minnesota. With Marley and Mary living near Minneapolis, and the Twin Cities metro area a rich source of employment possibilities after completion of my law degree, we picked Minnesota. Our plans were taking shape.

But still, I found myself anguishing over whether law school might be a mistake. Yes, a lawyer helped people deal with conflict in a constructive way. But at the end of the day, isn't the law premised on the capacity of the sheriff to enforce court orders? The law is fundamentally coercive, I said to myself, and my church has taught me to be nonresistant. What room is there for coercion among the nonresistant? And if I enter a group where coercion is routine, will my commitment to nonviolence soon wither and die?

These were questions straight out of my *Kleine Gemeinde* heritage, even though I didn't know it then. And yes, they would have said my anguish was the work of God's spirit in my life, warning me against sin.

I visited a local attorney, a Christian who attended the same Methodist congregation Sharon and I attended, and asked him my questions. He found them incomprehensible. I recalled conversations with Ed Diller, a Mennonite friend attending Harvard Law and planning to graduate later that spring. He recognized ethical challenges in the practice of law but didn't see membership in the bar to be one of them.

Although not at peace about this, I went ahead and began classes at the University of Minnesota.

Perhaps two months later, Mennonite theologian John H. Yoder visited our home while in Minneapolis to speak at a conference. At the request of the local Mennonite pastor, I picked Yoder up from the airport and we had a short time together over coffee. During my struggles with the question of whether I should study law, I had read some of Yoder's writings. He was a giant among Mennonite scholars, had a national reputation, and was an intimidating conversation partner. Having already begun my classes, I hesitated to disclose my indecision. Nevertheless, Yoder helped me. He expressed interest in my studies, my motivation for studying law, and my goals. And he said, "We need more young Mennonites in the field of law."

That's exactly what I needed to hear!

As I recall, he went on to say that because of our tradition and theology, Mennonites practicing law might see possibilities that others don't so readily see in how to work with conflict. He wasn't at all specific, and I didn't press him for more.

Looking back now, I think Yoder advised me wisely. My doubts about joining the legal ranks were rooted in my separatist past where distance and isolation had come to be seen as the way to enter the circle of God's grace. But that emphasis on separation is not our entire story. It wasn't there at the beginning in the Low Countries or even in Poland, especially not for city dwellers. Yoder seemed to assume that if I were serious about my faith, I would bring it with me into the legal profession. There, it would enable me to pursue forms of practice that lawyers from other backgrounds failed to fully appreciate.

The mistake I nearly made was to divide too sharply the gray and muddled world of the professions from the Kingdom of God. Had I persisted in that error, I either would have dropped out of law school or I would have pursued the profession's charms with a vengeance, claiming all the rewards I could while maintaining a separate religious sphere for spiritual matters.

Looking back now, I believe God's circle of grace includes those who enter conflict in the expectation that God is there, loving friend and enemy alike, nudging all toward candor, trust and reconciliation. When I am walking in the light, that becomes my job description too.

Educating our Children

Dad stopped attending school after 8th grade but his education wasn't finished. He expected it to be a life-long process and that's what it turned out to be. He learned how to install electrical wires and switches, sell cars and farm machinery, and master the many skills required of a farmer. Most of his adult education occurred on the job, but occasionally he attended a class or seminar. When I was in junior high, he enrolled in a weeknight Dale Carnegie course in Windom and learned how to stand before people and make a speech. I have the pen he won one evening for "best speech of the night."

Bible study was another aspect of informal education. Here Mom exceeded Dad but both made understanding the Bible a life-long project.

They valued formal education too and sent each of us boys off to college after high school. We weren't the first generation to seek higher education; two of Dad's siblings (Pete and Esther) earned college credits and two of Mom's completed college, Ed as an electrical engineer and Marcella as a teacher. That was ample precedent for us.

In regard to education, Mom and Dad had a blue-collar mind set: get enough formal education to get the kind of job you want. After that, let native intelligence and hard work take care of the rest. The status of the schools we attended didn't count much with them. In fact, it was almost the reverse: the more prestigious the educational institution, the more likely it would pull us away from the values we had been taught.

For good or ill, Sharon and I reflected many of the same attitudes when we made educational choices for our children. The decisions we made after moving from Minneapolis to Lancaster illustrate what I mean. Amber was twelve that summer; Emily was ten. After settling in to our Clay Street row-house, we visited the offices of the Lancaster City School District and enrolled our daughters in public schools.

We don't recall much preparation for this decision. We made a point of conferring with Rich and Martha Sider, friends whose daughters attended city schools. They told us of many fine teachers working there and that students with good support from home were well-prepared for college or university. Thus reassured, we proceeded. We'd chosen to live in the city, in part because we wanted to interact with the ethnic and political diversity of American life. It seemed natural to give our children the same opportunity through their school experiences.

Amber and Emily struggled some but made friends and did well academically. Each participated in school sports and in community athletic teams during the summer. I don't want to make it sound easy for them; it wasn't. They experienced the painful cliques of junior high school life, the scary rivalries among ethnic groups, and the social pressures to conform in order to be popular. But generally, Sharon and I understood the intensity of their struggles to be within the norm.

Amber completed high school in the city schools, graduating from McCaskey in 1995. Emily had every intention of doing the same but ran into difficulty during her 9th grade due to a friendship gone sour. With our support, she transferred to Lancaster Mennonite High School at the start of her sophomore year and graduated in 1997. We asked them to attend a Mennonite college for at least two years after high school graduation. Each agreed and each graduated from the college where she began, Amber from Goshen and Emily from Eastern Mennonite.

In short, our immediate family favored the public schools as the place for education but resorted to private schools as a back-up. Key factors in our decision-making were the adequacy of preparation for life-long learning and a social environment that would prepare our children for the world they would encounter when adults.

In the rural environment of my youth, most education-related discussion focused on which college to attend. There were few education-related decisions to make before that point. Nowadays, the choice of an elementary school seems to generate as much or more attention from parents. Sometimes such attention is rooted in the desire for children to get a fast start in the race toward the top of the social and economic pyramid. For those not concerned with social climbing, other factors weigh more heavily: friendship patterns, avoiding excessive peer pressure related to sexual activity and drugs, concern about a curriculum that is likely to affirm American exceptionalism and militarism, and the opportunity to let one's light shine (as we would have said it as children) within a very important community setting. In response to this mix of factors, some parents in Sharon's and my congregation here in Lancaster choose private schools, some home-school, and some continue to choose public schools.

It's interesting to reflect on how our extended family has responded to educational choices. In Sharon's and my generation, all seven children graduated from a public school, although in Sharon's family, the older children attended a private Bible school during some of their elementary years. Of the twelve children in Amber's and Emily's generation, seven graduated from a public school and five from a private high school. Of the sixteen school-age children in the following generation, ten are in public schools and six are being home-schooled.

Looking further back in our family's history, we see this issue was important in Russia during the 1860s, when the government began insisting on a larger role in the Mennonite schools. In the U.S., it receded in importance when our ancestors lived in rural communities where they felt connected to local school administrators and able to influence the classroom environment.[12] But whenever propaganda and indoctrination become dominant on school agendas, or whenever the authority of families is diminished on critical matters, the issue rightly reemerges: who are the people to whom we give the authority to educate our children and shape their view of the world?

Marriage and Church

Marriage involves becoming a member of a new group: a new family, to be sure, and often a community beyond that. Sometimes this leads a family to change directions. One example of this occurred in 1807 when Helena Friesen, the 20-year-old daughter of Abraham and Margaretha von Riesen, married Klaas Reimer, a 37-year-old minister, farmer and widower from Petershagen in Molotschna Colony.

As indicated earlier, in the Russian colonies the Mennonites had responsibility for all of their local affairs. They had to decide how to deal with issues of public drunkenness, fighting and theft. Of course, such behavior also had been present in Poland too, but there the roles between the government and the church had been clearly separated.

Local officials who generally were not Mennonites arrested and punished those who broke the law; if a lawbreaker were part of a congregation, then that group dealt with repentance (change of heart) and restoration.

In Molotschna, each village had a mayor, who deputized individuals on a rotating basis to act as police officers and keep the peace. These officers arrested lawbreakers, held them in a secure facility, and punished them, usually with a leather whip called a *knute.* Above them was a super-mayor with responsibility for keeping the peace across the entire Colony. All of these people were Mennonites.

There were lots of problems with the administration of this system, as one would expect in a settlement only a few years old. What became most problematic was figuring out the relationship between the so-called civil authorities and the church. Mennonite church leaders regarded themselves as the highest authorities in the community, especially at the beginning of the Colony's history. But by asserting this authority, they also assumed responsibility for coercive arrests, jailings, and beatings. For a group long committed to nonviolence, this created profound dissonance.

As the highest authority, the church leaders also became the destination for the inevitable raft of grievances against village administrators and police officers. Had a whipping been unjust? Had too many blows been struck? Those issues ended up at next week's church meeting. And in some of those meetings, the participants ended up in fist fights.

Klaas Reimer criticized this system. He argued that congregational leaders should be using scriptural methods such as teaching, counseling, loss of membership, shunning, and restoration to enforce discipline in the congregation. More typically, however, church leaders ignored bad behavior by referring the individuals involved to village administrators to deal with, in which case the problem was no longer framed by scriptural teachings but by force and punishment. That, said Reimer, was wrong.[13]

Reimer's second major rift with the Colony's church leaders concerned the collection of financial support for the Russian government in its wars against Napoleon. Reimer's elder (the overseer) circulated a pledge sheet to landowners so individuals could indicate how much they were willing to contribute. Reimer opposed this involvement of the church in the collection of funds for war.

In 1812, Reimer began to host separate worship services in private homes in Petershagen. Initially, he hoped this step would precipitate constructive conversations leading to reform within the church that had appointed him to be a minister. But the separate meetings only served to widen the split and in 1814, the group under Reimer's leadership constituted themselves as a separate body. The broader community mocked them by calling them the *Kleine Gemeinde*, or little church, and the name stuck.

Reimer's problems continued and the Colony's leaders twice threatened him with exile to Siberia. The *Kleine Gemeinde* was not accepted by the *Gross Gemeinde* as a legitimate church until 1843, and then only at the order of the Russian civil authorities.

All of this controversy entered Abraham Friesen's life too, simply because his sister, Helena, was Reimer's wife. Gradually, Abraham became convinced his brother-in-law had it right. In 1818, just a year after being selected as a deacon by the *Gross Gemeinde,* Abraham joined the *Kleine Gemeinde.* After Reimer's death, Friesen became the group's leading elder, a role he filled for nine years.

As previously noted, the *Kleine Gemeinde* were the "old order" of the Dutch-Prussian-Russian branch of Mennonites. Their austere lifestyle, plain dress, and avoidance of frivolous speech and humor set them apart from others. Starting with Abraham Friesen and continuing for nearly 100 years, this old order tradition was woven into my heritage. And it all began with a wedding, when Helena married Klaas.

*****

My grandparents, George and Elizabeth Friesen, married in March 1906. The wedding occurred at the *Bruderthaler* congregation in Jansen, Nebraska where Elizabeth's father, Heinrich Ratzlaff, was pastor. He led the couple through their wedding vows, which included spoken prayers by the bride and groom. For George, who had been raised and baptized among the *Kleine Gemeinde,* it was his first experience praying aloud.

The decision of the couple to marry in the *Bruderthaler* church was a turning point in the Friesen family's story. It meant, first of all, their adoption of that more open congregation as their primary community. Secondly, it meant they would not leave Nebraska with the *Kleine Gemeinde*, which were about to pull up stakes and start yet again at a new location.

The factors that made Jefferson County, Nebraska economically attractive to the Mennonite immigrants (good soil, adequate rainfall, proximity to markets) also attracted others. Throughout the 1880s, the County's lands continued to fill with settlers. This meant less land for inexpensive purchase by Mennonite families, who needed expansion if their children were to continue the traditional farming life. Under the pressure of a growing population and rising prices, farms became smaller. In 1880 the average acreage per farm among the Mennonites was 208; by 1900, it had fallen to 133 and an increasing number of young families owned no land at all.

Faced with a shortage of inexpensive land, as well as concerns about the attractiveness of evangelical churches and secular entertainments in town, the *Kleine Gemeinde* congregation again began to consider relocation. After a period of discernment, it voted to relocate to a place where land was more plentiful and inexpensive. They seriously considered a site in Saskatchewan but eventually agreed on an area in western Kansas near Meade. In September 1906, after selling their lands and packing their furnishings and equipment in railroad cars, the migration began.

In 1908, my great-grandparents Gerhard and Helena Friesen joined the move to the west Kansas plains. Gerhard was 45 at the time; Helena was 44. They were accompanied by three of their four married children and their five minor children.

George was the only member of Gerhard and Helena's family to stay in Nebraska. With his new wife, he worshipped with the *Bruderthaler* congregation, a group that later joined the Evangelical Mennonite Brethren conference, until 1933. Then, on the occasion of my father's baptism as a teenager into the Jansen Mennonite Brethren Church, George and Elizabeth asked to be rebaptized and also joined the Mennonite Brethren.

Although Grandpa gained a new community when he married Grandma, he also lost the economic strength of the old one. Because he did not live near extended family, George no longer had a land base and easy access to animal power, breeding stock, farm equipment, volunteer labor, and inexpensive capital. Instead, the American style of self-reliance and commercial credit became his path. As the years unfolded and the contingencies of life occurred, the separation from the support of the *Kleine Gemeinde* took a heavy economic toll. Due to his financial difficulties, Grandpa lost one farm in 1923 and another in 1939. When my parents and brothers visited Grandpa and Grandma in California in 1947, he was 61 and working as a janitor in a large elementary school.

*****

Two of Mom's siblings became Roman Catholic though marriage. Aunt Charlotte married Clarence Prokop in 1948; Uncle Ted married Gladys Maras in 1956.

Those Catholics were tough. For the priest to be involved or the church building used in the wedding, the non-Catholic had to agree to become Catholic and raise the hoped-for children in the Catholic Church. Back in the days when our families lived in Prussia and Poland, Mennonites were tough like that too. "Do it our way or you'll be shunned." But by the 20th century, we had become much more flexible.

Mom struggled to come to terms with the fact that two of her siblings were Roman Catholic, two mainline Protestant, and two nothing at all. Only she and Uncle Harold remained in the Mennonite church of their birth. What was she to make of the others? She filled her prayers with intercession for them.

At Easter in 1991, LeRoy and Sharryl joined the Roman Catholic Church. Sharryl previously had been a member of Swedish Covenant and Mennonite congregations while LeRoy had always been Mennonite. So it wasn't the priest twisting any arms in their case; they chose to be Catholic. At any rate, since their Easter induction, they have largely moved in Roman Catholic rather than Mennonite circles.

LeRoy has written about this and explained the reasons for their decision. It was precipitated by their mid-life divorces. But it was rooted in their appreciation for Catholic rituals of worship and their desire to be part of a body that goes all the way back to the beginning and has, through all the zigzags of the carnal and the sublime, continued to reconcile its differences into one coherent body. In other words, the Roman Catholic way of dealing with conflict is different than the Mennonites' way, which usually involves splintering and division.

As I indicated, Mom's siblings unknowingly prepared her for LeRoy and Sharryl's decision. She accepted it with grace and characteristic curiosity.

What I find most interesting about the Catholics is their politics. They have a commitment to life and against abortion that has shaped the political life of this country. Pro-choice John Kerry lost in 2004 because so many Catholics deviated from their usual practice and voted Republican. Indeed, along with the evangelicals who joined their cause in the early '80s, the Catholic tenacity on the abortion issue has shifted the entire culture in a pro-life direction. Without agreeing to every aspect of their advocacy or with all the results, I laud their achievement. They have accomplished something a bit like what the Anabaptists achieved in the 16th Century: convincing people who aren't Roman Catholic that something valuable is at stake, something that must be respected.

Of course, fundamentalist and evangelical Protestant churches also have become overtly political since the 1980s when television preachers began organizing them into a potent force for the Republican Party. I don't admire this and don't see it as similar to what the Anabaptists did or what the Roman Catholics are still doing. Instead, I perceive the connection between their religious beliefs and their political advocacy to lack integrity and consistency. Let me try to explain.

Roman Catholics provide significant support for the pro-life agenda as it relates to the minimum wage, labor organizing, health care, the social safety net, food security, the treatment of prisoners, and the needs of immigrants. A few notable Catholics even oppose war as a part of the pro-life agenda. But among fundamentalist and evangelical Protestant churches, the pro-life agenda often has stopped with abortion. That's why I tend to be skeptical of their insistence that opposition to abortion is rooted in their faith. I'm inclined to see it instead as based in their politics, which always comes first.

The point is that faith-based groups can shape culture in a positive way.[14] For people like me who believe the Kingdom of God is an earthly phenomenon always shaping our world, it's instructive to be around groups of people, such as the Catholics, who also believe this and are actually doing it.

*****

We know little about the church affiliations of the Klassen clan when they first arrived in Minnesota. In Russia, Gerhard and Maria had been part of the *Rudnerweide* congregation, a group affiliated with the *Gross Gemeinde*. During their early years in Minnesota, they probably attended the congregation that met on the hill north of Mountain Lake and later became known as Gospel Mennonite. In 1889, after a dispute over the introduction of Sunday school led to a split in the congregation, the Klassens, including Gerhard and Maria, probably became part of the newly formed *Bruderthaler* group, later known as the Evangelical Mennonite Brethren (EMB). Youngest daughter Anna's husband, Peter Schultz, preached there and pulled the entire family in that direction.

If Sharon's great-grandfather Abraham had not died prematurely, it is likely he and his family also would have joined that congregation. Certainly his wife, Elizabeth, had a background that would have supported such a decision. She had received instruction and baptism at age sixteen from August Lenzmann, the influential Russian elder and teacher who led the *Gnadenfeld* congregation and incorporated teachings from Lutheran evangelists and authors. Lenzmann had close and frequent contacts with the individuals who in 1860 broke away from the *Gross Gemeinde* and formed the Mennonite Brethren. But he never joined himself. It would have been consistent with this history for Elizabeth to associate herself with the EMBs, a group similar in many ways to the *Gnadenfeld* congregation she had first joined in Russia.

But by the time the EMB church started, Elizabeth had already associated herself with the Mennonite Brethren Church, which required a second baptism because of its teaching that the first, done by sprinkling or pouring water on the head, had not been biblically sufficient. This turn of events may have been linked to her marriage in 1881 to Heinrich Flaming, who had not been a church member back in Russia. Together, in 1885 Elizabeth and Heinrich joined the Mountain Lake Mennonite Brethren congregation, which is where her grandson, Will, met his future wife, Esther, fifty years later.

That's how Sharon came to be raised in the Mennonite Brethren Church. And that helps explain why growing up, Sharon didn't know she had lots of Klassen cousins in town. They went to a different church!

Church and Community

At age 11, in the lake near Mountain Lake, I was baptized into the Carson Mennonite Brethren Church by Rev. G. S. Warkentin. It was the congregation Mom had been raised in and both of her parents had been raised in. Mom's grandfather had been a minister there for 33 years.

But when the Wienses first immigrated, they – like nearly all of Sharon's and my ancestors -- were part of the mainline Mennonite group in Russia, not the breakaway Mennonite Brethren.

On the first Sunday of February, 1877, my great-great-grandparents, Jacob and Anna Wiens, invited other nearby Mennonite immigrant families to their farm home for worship and fellowship. Five couples joined them that first Sunday, four of them Mennonite Brethren.[15] We can imagine that Jacob led the worship. He knew his Bible well, had served as a minister in Russia, and had counseled others regarding faith.

The group continued meeting and began to think of themselves as a congregation. Another four couples joined them. When spring arrived, they added an afternoon service for the children.

On two Sundays in June, seven adults were baptized, two for the first time and five for the second. They conducted the ritual in the Mennonite Brethren way, by immersion, meaning the entire bodies of those baptized were submerged in the water. Jacob was among the five rebaptized. He was fifty-six at the time; the man who baptized him was a thirty-three year old layman, Peter Martens. The event took place at either Eagle Lake or Long Lake.

I wish I knew more about why Jacob took this step. Perhaps during Bible study with his Mennonite Brethren neighbors he became convinced immersion was the correct form of baptism.[16] Or perhaps he knew that without rebaptism, he would not have full fellowship with his neighbors.

Two of the founding members, Peter and Maria Penner, declined the invitation to be rebaptized. Instead, they joined a General Conference Mennonite congregation in Mountain Lake. Their grandson became the first overseas missionary to be commissioned by that Conference. I mention this sign of the Penners' commitment to the Gospel because in 1977, I joined a General Conference congregation, thus making a U-turn in the path Jacob Wiens struck a century earlier.

Growing up, Sharon and I had friends from families that attended General Conference congregations. But our parents rarely mixed socially and we kids did not have much opportunity to be in one another's homes. The difference in baptismal styles was hooked to other theological differences: they emphasized good works in daily life, we emphasized the good work of being born again. Each group believed its own views were right and each group felt annoyed at the other's self-righteous attitude. It didn't make for frequent collaboration among our congregations or close friendships among our parents.

*****

As I imagine it is with most children, growing up required me to make sense of the bewildering ebb and flow of parental judgments about whom I was permitted to associate with socially and whom I was not. Because of our Mennonite heritage, this was a particularly important matter. If we got it wrong, we would end up living just like everyone else and our witness to Jesus Christ would be lost.

As a boy, I occasionally climbed to the top of our barn roof, stood alongside the tin cupola, and surveyed the surrounding countryside. I could see perhaps fifteen other farmyards. As best I can recollect, all but one was occupied by a Mennonite family that had reached the United States at the same time and via the same general route as my family.

Most were members of the same congregation as my family. And about half those neighbors were related in one way or another to my mother.

In 1954, the bachelor farmer just to the south of us died due to an accident while he was unloading grain alone late at night. His farm was put up for public sale and Dick and Dorothy Espenson, a family from Sleepy Eye, bought it. Though they knew little about the Mennonites, the Espenson family started attending our church.

Dad helped them move in on his 37th birthday. He was delighted to have them as neighbors because they were Christians but not encumbered by all our Mennonite traditions. Dad and Dick exchanged labor and equipment, jokes and sorrows. Our two families often socialized together. As I watched Dad interact with the Espenson family, I concluded it was a good thing to break out of our Mennonite circle and make friends with people from backgrounds different than our own.

It wasn't just Dad who was happy to have new neighbors; the Espenson family made a positive impact on our whole family. Their oldest daughter was Marley's age, their youngest daughter my age, and in between were twin sons. One could say they were our first "American friends" and we tried to make them feel welcome in our Mennonite neighborhood.

Here's an example of what I mean. Because our homes were so close, we were part of the same telephone party line, which linked six or seven residences together. This meant only one residence could place a call at a time and all linked residences could listen in to the conversations initiated on other telephones. Everyone agreed proper etiquette required one not listen to someone else's conversation. But most everyone listened anyway.

Mom and Dad's first language was *plautdietsch,* a dialect of the German language. It emerged during the many years Mennonites lived in Poland, which was primarily a Low German-speaking environment. It also included elements of other languages, especially Dutch and later Polish, Ukrainian and English.

When Mom talked to extended family members or friends on the phone, she usually spoke *plautdietsch.* It was familiar and it was fun. But Dad asked her to stop doing that. "You're shutting out our new neighbors when you do that," he said. "It sets up a barrier between us." Mom reluctantly complied; discontinuing use of one's favorite language is no small thing, especially in a venue that is supposed to be private.

Later, when in junior high school, I received a very different message from my parents. I was making new friends and not all of them were Mennonites. One was from a Lutheran family. His church planned to have a hayride party for their youth and he invited me to join. I was pleased as punch until I mentioned the invitation to my parents. They told me I could not accept. "Why not?" I asked incredulously. The answer was vague and unsatisfying. What I took from it is that they didn't want me hanging out with Lutheran kids.

To be fair, I didn't hang out with youth groups from other Mennonite churches either. Still, my parents' actions seemed arbitrary and judgmental. I wondered: if the Espenson family had been true to their Danish roots and attended a Lutheran congregation instead of our church, would we have spent so much time with them?

Sharon has her own story along these lines. Jane, her best friend in junior high school, was from a Lutheran family. Sharon and Jane spent a lot of time in each other's homes. In this respect, I wish my family had been more like the Klassens.

*****

Although my great-grandparents, Gerhard and Helena Friesen, moved to western Kansas along with other members of the *Kleine Gemeinde,* their association with that group soon drew to a close. In 1913, after only five years in Kansas, they moved back to Jansen, Nebraska where they enjoyed the company of old neighbors and friends. Some of their children accompanied them to Nebraska; others stayed back in Kansas.

In 1917, Gerhard and Helena moved yet again, back to western Kansas and the town of Montezuma, where they operated a creamery. They began attending a Church of God, Mennonite (Holdeman) congregation, which rebaptized them in June of that year. There they spent their final years. Gerhard died in 1930 at age 67; Helena died that same year at age 66.

Yet a tenuous Friesen family connection to the *Kleine Gemeinde* continued beyond their rebaptisms and final passing. A daughter, Anna, married and raised a family in the *Kleine Gemeinde* congregation near Meade. One of her sons, George Isaac, turned his inventive genius into Meade Manufacturing, a prominent local employer during the '50s and '60s. Gerhard's half-brother, Abram E. Friesen, and his wife, Katherine Reimer, immigrated to Chihuahua, Mexico during the early 1920s to help start a *Kleine Gemeinde* colony there. Some of their descendants later migrated to colonies in Bolivia. So yes, even today, a few members of the larger Friesen family continue in fellowship with that group.

As for the *Kleine Gemeinde* congregation in western Kansas, membership grew steadily for the first three decades, reaching a high point of 275 adults in the late '30s. Then came the stress of conscription during World War II and growing interest among members in the music, outreach practices, and enthusiasm of evangelical churches. When the elder, Jacob F. Isaac, held the line, discontent intensified. In 1943, a petition circulated among the members calling for a merger with the *Bruderthaler* (Evangelical Mennonite Brethren) group in Meade. It received strong support. Thus, the nearly 70-year history of the *Kleine Gemeinde* in the United States ended.

*****

As old patterns of kinship, village life, and communitarian faith melt away like snow under the spring sun, people face a choice. Do they find new forms of social cohesion that enable the living out of old values in new ways? Or do they go it alone, managing to stay afloat on whatever currents swirl around them?

The exercise of these choices is found throughout my Friesen family's story. Among most of the individuals described here, we see movement first from the *Kleine Gemeinde* to the Evangelical Mennonite Brethren, and then from the Evangelical Mennonite Brethren to the Mennonite Brethren. Each step involved the pain of severed fellowship and the shame of admitting one's past expression of faith had been half-hearted and legalistic. Yet each step also provided rewards: stronger assurances of salvation, a more emotionally expressive faith, and new opportunities to participate in and engage the world. Judging by the accounts noted here, many viewed it as an attractive exchange.

As noted above, a few disdained that path and have remained in the *Kleine Gemeinde* to this day. Many more have little interest in trying to "get it right" by finding a better church or more faithful expression of their commitments; they have come to understand their lives in a different way, without religious affiliation. By and large, the stories of that choice are not told here because it has not been Sharon's and my choice nor the historical choice of our families. But we will return to that option in Chapter 5.

During the late '40s and '50s, my parents, along with their siblings and many other rural Mennonites, faced these choices. Though my parents never changed churches, they attempted a transition that honored their ancestors' commitments yet expressed them in new ways.

Royden Loewen, a scholar whose family roots are in the *Kleine Gemeinde*, describes this transition as finding a way to "stand apart in the world" while also accommodating modern trends. He documented this move in two communities: Meade, Kansas and Steinbach, Manitoba.

In both, evangelicalism was the chosen path. Loewen identifies the boundary markers of this newly-adopted subculture: the importance of being "saved" and leading others to salvation; beliefs related to the virgin birth, the inspiration of scripture and the escape (rapture) of Christians into heaven; abstinence from the use of alcohol and tobacco; and anticommunism. As they began to feel secure in this new subculture, Mennonites let go of traditional boundary markers (traditional dress, German language, refusal to participate in the military) that seemed only to impede their economic, social and political integration.

How did this embrace of evangelicalism help rural Mennonites "stand apart in the world" while also accommodating modern trends? Loewen answers:

> "It provided for a stable pathway out of the agrarian community for it now associated the concept of 'world' not so much with a wider geography, but with a licentious lifestyle. Now the one-time sectarians were armed with a religious language and cosmology that not only had currency in the wider world but made a sustained interaction with that world a social imperative."[17]

Loewen's analysis explains why I often was confused as a child by the judgments my parents made. Dad and Mom were sincere in wanting to break out of their ethnic enclave and become more accepting and welcoming of others. But they also wanted to continue thinking of themselves as people "standing apart from the world." So they erected new barriers, defined by the evangelical subculture, especially with regard to our youthful friendships and associations.

Looking back, I see that Sharon and I attempted something very similar, only with Anabaptism as our source of boundary markers. Through the group identities we embraced and those we avoided, we have attempted to stand apart from the world, much as our parents did.

I feel no chagrin about this. It is true that group membership creates identities that can separate and divide. It also is true these divisions can generate conflict. Yet so long as we yearn for love, beauty and justice, conflict will be our companion. We can avoid it only by joining the apathetic and the anaesthetized.

Indeed, this understanding is a core part of the identity we have received from our ancestors. We are partisans in the great unfolding of God's purposes in this world. This leaves us vulnerable to all of the errors that bedevil the committed: closed-mindedness, group-think, prejudice, fear and violence. Those errors, grievous as they are, still pale before distortions all around that threaten to extinguish our humanity. In part, this is why our ancestors chose to be partisans and it is why we are called to make the same choice.

Yes, our heritage calls each of us to be peaceful. But more than that, it calls us to become part of a people of peace.[18] In that seemingly small distinction lies a great political difference.

*****

During my first year of law school, Sharon and I started attending Faith Mennonite Church in Minneapolis. That congregation encouraged its members to join informal fellowship groups meeting in private homes. In the spring of 1977, Sharon and I did that, even though Amber was still a baby and I a busy law student. The group we joined met weekly.

One of our activities as a group was reading *Life Together,* the classic by Lutheran martyr Dietrich Bonhoeffer. In 1935, at a time when the Nazi regime in Germany was shutting down religious activities that were not supportive of its agenda, Bonhoeffer accepted the leadership of an illegal and clandestine seminary in the German province of Pomerania. There he shared a communal life with other teachers and students. Out of this experience he wrote *Life Together* and described the sustaining and imaginative power of that fellowship among the beleaguered teachers and students.

One of my strong memories of those years relates to how the group responded to me as a law student. Attending the University of Minnesota Law School was an intense experience for me. As an undergrad, I had attended tiny Tabor College, which had no pre-law program. I had been away from formal education for six years, and my family background had provided no context for my studies. I was intimidated, yet also was enjoying a measure of success. The place of this country bumpkin among my classmates was beginning to emerge and it wasn't so shabby. It was a heady time for me.

Within our evening fellowship meetings, I had a share of the agenda to talk about my life. But the group was not about me. It was first about God, then about the fellowship we shared, and then about each of us as individuals in equal measure. Without a word of rebuke, the experience chastened my vanity and pride. It began to teach me a lesson I still am learning: the pathway to the full expression of my gifts and abilities is in the company of others whose first attention is directed elsewhere.

Bonhoeffer wrote about our resistance to this lesson in *Life Together*.

> "Sin demands to have a man by himself. It withdraws him from the community. The more isolated a person is, the more destructive will be the power of sin over him, and the more deeply he becomes involved in it, the more disastrous is his isolation. Sin wants to remain unknown. It shuns the light."[19]

Throughout the law school experience, where striving for achievement and positioning for status dominated my days, this group quietly and without drama kept my feet on the ground. Without it, a sense of entitlement would have gotten the best of me and our marriage. Without it, I wouldn't have accepted an invitation in the summer of 1978 to work in a storefront law clinic. Without it, I wouldn't have begun to understand how our understanding of God and our view of the world depends on which people we give authority to shape our lives.

A Post-modern Anxiety

We are wishful thinkers,
seeing what we look for
hearing what we want to hear.
And so we strive for distance
thus to see things as they really are.

Yet those exploring space inside the atom
tracking particles too small to see
tell of a conundrum at the center of things.
Reality from a distance differs from reality up close;
relationship serves, unbidden, to shape what is.

History provides a similar lesson;
think of the time Romans ruled the world.
Believers touched flesh
of the resurrected Jesus;
skeptics apparently saw no one at all.

This is creation without hard edges:
squishy, elusive,
never quite set.
Giving us what we yearn for
denying what we choose to ignore.

---

[1] Donne, John. "An Anatomy of the World", 1611.

[2] Bellah, Robert N., Richard Madsen, William M. Sullivan, Ann Swindler and Steven M. Tipton. *Habits of the Heart,* Harper & Row, 1985 at 286.

[3] While involvement in national political life has been rare in our families, a few have been active in state and local electoral politics. Johann P. Thiessen, a first cousin of my great-great-grandfather Jacob L. Friesen, won two terms in the Nebraska state legislature. A great-great uncle, Peter Wiens, won elections for Cottonwood County commissioner. Both Dad and Marley won school board elections in Mountain Lake. In 2003, LeRoy and Carol's daughter, Tiffany, lost a closely contested race

for school board in Atlanta, Georgia. Only Thiessen was a politician in the conventional sense. His transformation from *Kleine Gemeinde* immigrant in 1874 to merchant and banker in the 1880s, state legislator in 1909, and chairman of the local Council for the Defense of America in 1917 is described by Royden Loewen in *Diaspora in the Countryside: Two Mennonite Communities and Mid-Twentieth-Century Rural Disjuncture,* University of Illinois Press, 2006

[4] Art Hershey, Randy Wenger, Merle Good, Duane Shank respectively.

[5] Loewen, Harry. *No Permanent City: Stories from Mennonite History and Life,* Herald Press, 1993.

[6] Quoted in *No Permanent City: Stories from Mennonite History and Life,* Herald Press, 1993.at 81.

[7] Klassen, *Mennonites in Early Modern Poland & Prussia,* at 173.

[8] Bender, Elizabeth H. "Ernst von Wildenbruch's Drama Der Menonit." *Mennonite Quarterly Review* XVIII (1944): 22-35.

[9] Hershberger, Guy F., Albert N. Keim and Hanspeter Jecker. “Conscientious Objection.” *Global Anabaptist Mennonite Encyclopedia Online,* 1989.

[10] G. S. Warkentin and Loyal Martin.

[11] Jesus enacted this invitation by refusing to mount a violent defense against his opponents. This tells us something important about the way of God, who extends forgiveness to enemies instead of retaliation and thereby seeks to restore those who are estranged.

[12] During those first decades in Minnesota, Mennonite families established a network of private “German schools” as an alternative to public education. This development was fueled by a state law that forbid the teaching of the Bible in public schools. By the late 1890s attitudes had changed and several Mennonites became leaders in the public system. However, private education has always remained an option in Mt. Lake. See *Jublilee Celebration – The Mennonite Settlement in Mountain Lake, Minnesota 1875-1925,* supra.

13 Plett, Delbert F. *Saints and Sinners – The Kleine Gemeinde in Imperial Russia*, Crossway Publications, 1999, at 47-49.

[14] Zionism has convinced many Jews that for their witness to endure, it needs a Jewish state and the coercive power of government. But this is a recent development; for centuries, the Jews of the diaspora showed us that a minority subculture can both endure and have a positive, transforming impact on the dominant society.

[15] Friedrich and Aganetha Strauss, Heinrich and Anna Boldt, Daniel and Katrina Bergthold, Peter and Maria Martens, and Peter and Maria Penner. See *80th Anniversary 1877-1957,* a pamphlet published by the Mennonite Brethren Churches of Delft and Mountain Lake, Minnesota, 1957.

[16] Those who rebaptized Jacob likely said he had been saved from his formerly lost condition. Perhaps Jacob also said that. Such comments reflected badly on one's former fellowship and contributed much to the ill-will between members of the two Mennonite groups.

[17] *Loewen, Diaspora in the Countryside: Two Mennonite Communities and Mid-Twentieth-Century Rural Disjuncture, at 101.*

[18] Jesus began with an invitation to join a group (his disciples). Our partisan identity can begin with an induction ceremony called baptism.

[19] Bonhoeffer, Dietrich. *Life Together*, Harper & Row, 1954 at 96, 112.

"Hope has two beautiful daughters;
their names are Anger and Courage.
Anger at the way things are;
Courage to make them as they ought to be."[1]
St. Augustine of Hippo

Chapter 4: When will we dissent?

Our ancestors communicated dissent from prevailing cultural or political norms by their nonconformity. When that expression of dissent was not permitted, they packed their bags and moved to another place.

One may argue flight isn't dissent. Under this view, only those who stay behind and persist in their nonconformity deserve this badge of honor. To cite an historical example, only those who accepted induction into the military during World War I but then refused to wear the uniform demonstrated the courage we usually associate with dissent. They publicly refused to conform and then accepted the consequences of their actions.

The differences in theology and worldview between those who flee and those who stay behind and resist are important to think about. But in my view, both actions can be ways of bearing witness to one's ultimate allegiance. Each demonstrates an alternative to whatever brand of orthodoxy the powers seek to impose. Insofar as such acts are claimed by the church and explained to the public as faithful acts of witness, they create new options and demonstrate again why the story of Jesus Christ is called "good news."

This chapter will describe a few instances of dissent in our family, one by flight and the others by staying in place. It is a short chapter because the record of such activity is short. As we move into an era when dissent will be an increasingly important aspect of bearing witness to hope, we should focus on this vital question, even if our families have little to offer by way of inspiration.

Midnight Train to Canada

In mid-May 1917, Isaac Voth, his brother Abram, and their cousin, Jacob H. Wiens, packed suitcases for a trip of unknown duration to Canada. The three men were in their twenties and unmarried, although Wiens had a sweetheart and was planning soon to wed. They left quietly, almost secretly; there were no family picnics to say farewell, no prayers of blessing at the front of the church. In the middle of the night, Isaac's and Abram's father, the long-serving and highly regarded elder of the two Mennonite Brethren congregations in Cottonwood County, drove them to the rail station in Bingham Lake. They boarded a train for the Twin Cities; later the next day, they arrived in Manitoba.

Isaac, Abram and John, members of the Mennonite Brethren Church in Carson Township, traveled to Canada to avoid conscription into the U.S. military for the so-called "war to end all wars."

The conscription law these young men avoided was signed into law by President Woodrow Wilson on May 18, 1917. It required every man at least 21 and less than 31 years of age to register with the U.S military. The law stated it was a misdemeanor to willfully fail to register or to help anyone else evade the requirement to register.

The American people did not want to join the war. Commentators often characterize this sentiment as "isolationist," a word meant to convey backwardness and the inability to comprehend how peoples and nations are connected. But popular sentiment was correct in this instance; World War I was a rash and pointless war and led directly to another world war that while easier to understand, was even more destructive.

Woodrow Wilson, the great liberal, won a second term in the White House by promising he would keep the United States out of the war. Then, securely back in the White House, he promptly broke his promise. In a speech delivered at about the time Jacob Wiens and his two cousins boarded the train in Bingham Lake, Wilson said the following.

> "The whole nation must be a team, in which each man shall play the part for which he is best fitted. To this end, Congress has provided that the nation shall be organized for war by selection; that each man shall be classified for service in the place to which it shall best serve the general good to call him.

"The significance of this cannot be overstated. It is a new thing in our history and a landmark in our progress. It is a new manner of accepting and vitalizing our duty to give ourselves with thoughtful devotion to the common purpose of us all. It is in no sense a conscription of the unwilling; it is selection from a nation which has volunteered in mass."

In Canada, Isaac married a niece of Sharon's mother; they lived in Manitoba the rest of their lives. Abram married a Canadian woman and they lived their years in Canada too. Jacob Wiens married his sweetheart from Carson, who followed him to Manitoba later in 1917. They lived in Manitoba until 1930 when it felt safe to return to the Mountain Lake area to be near their families without fear of prosecution. Their children were Mom's second cousins.

Although Jacob grew up across the field from the Balzers and was a first cousin of my grandfather Wiens, I first learned his story from his grandchildren, Jim and Mervin Dick, in 2008, over ninety years after it occurred. They found the story to be painful to relate, all those years later. Obviously, Jacob's congregation (the one I grew up in) did not embrace the decisions those young men had made. Somehow, a congregation whose ancestors had left Prussia and then Russia to avoid military service concluded these young men were draft-dodgers. Thus, their departure was stigmatized and their witness extinguished.

I can't help but wonder about the connection between the congregation's rejection of their witness and the participation of my uncles in war, a quarter century later.

In 1918, a year after the midnight train ride to Winnipeg, Isaac's and Abram's father, the Rev. Heinrich Voth, resigned his leadership of the two Mennonite Brethren congregations in Cottonwood County and moved to Canada. Did he fear prosecution? Had the congregations he led into national prominence turned against him? Did he simply want to be near his sons? I wish I knew the answer.

Agitation for Land Reform

As originally constituted by the Russian government agency responsible for settling immigrants, nearly one-quarter of the land in the Molotschna Colony was reserved for future allocations to new farming families. This plan was designed to accommodate what all expected to be a growing population. In the meantime, the existing farmers were allowed to lease these lands for nominal rent payments. As one would expect, the larger and more prosperous farmers took most advantage of this arrangement. At first, no one had a problem with any part of this.

But later, as the population grew, the context changed drastically. Families were large and each son needed a farm. Assuming an average of six sons per family surviving to adulthood, in two generations (50 years), a family on one farm would generate the need for 36 farms. Thus, it became necessary for Colony administrators to stop leasing the reserve lands to established farmers and begin allocating those fields to new farmers. That's where the problem got complicated. Only landowning males had the right to vote in Molotschna, and they opposed the allocation of reserve lands to the landless because it was highly profitable to rent those lands. Without landowner support, Colony administrators found it politically impossible to act in a just fashion.

By the 1860s, the situation had become critical. Around two-thirds of Colony residents were landless. Many were angry and agitation against the landowning class divided the Colony.

With no help coming from the Mennonite leadership of the Colony, the landless turned to Russian government officials for help. The problem received high-level attention, resulting in an Imperial Edict in 1866 requiring land reform in Molotschna. Again, however, the large landowners actively opposed the implementation of the edict and succeeded in blocking portions of the plan.

Abraham F. Thiessen, the grandson of *Kleine Gemeinde* elder Abraham W. Friesen, emerged in 1866 as a leading advocate for the landless. Thiessen was a merchant, landless himself, and a man of fiery temperament who had been expelled by the *Kleine Gemeinde* for his refusal to accept the discipline of his congregation. He publicly accused the landowners of bribing government officials in order to manipulate implementation of the imperial land reform plan. He wrote a book in which he highlighted the plight of the landless. And he began making repeated trips to the Russian capital in St. Petersburg to voice his accusations and to lobby government ministers on behalf of the landless.[2]

In 1873, Colony officials had him arrested and held in prison in Berdjansk. The following year, he was banished to a labor camp in Siberia. The historical record does not indicate what charges were brought against him but they were rooted in the accusation that he was creating dissension and causing the Colony to be held in disrepute.

In 1876, Thiessen bribed his way out of the Siberian labor camp and fled to Europe. From there he immigrated to the United States and settled in Jansen, Nebraska, where his son already lived. In 1887 he returned to Molotschna to again advocate for the landless. However, he was arrested soon after arrival and immediately deported. He died in Jansen in 1889 at age 52.

Mennonite historians are divided in their assessment of Thiessen. James Urry describes him as "a troublesome individual" who often failed to adequately substantiate his accusations. Cornelius Krahn considers him "among the prophets and fearless fighters. . . . who did influence the cause of justice and Christian love in a community that had almost forgotten what that was."[3] As for the impact of his efforts, that too was mixed. The plight of the landless improved during the 1860s, but chiefly through starting new colonies, not because of equitable distribution of reserve lands within Molotschna Colony.

Civil Disobedience

By and large, we have been a law-abiding family, Jacob H. Wiens and Abraham F. Thiessen notwithstanding. But I'm aware of two other acts of civil disobedience, both in my brother LeRoy's family.

In 1971, shortly before Dad died, LeRoy, his first wife, Carol, and their three children[4] moved to East Jerusalem to accept the leadership of Mennonite Central Committee's development and peace-building programs in the Middle East. In this role, they represented North American Mennonites and so traveled extensively in the region and developed working relationships and friendships with church leaders, aid agency executives, and activists. They worked primary with Palestinians but also formed relationship with Lebanese, Jordanians and Israelis whose lives had been marked by severe injustice and great loss. For a year during the Lebanese civil war, they lived in Beirut.

The experience of those years shaped LeRoy and Carol long after their return to the United States in the summer of 1976. In an April 15, 1978 letter to the western regional office of the Internal Revenue Service, they explained why they had not enclosed full payment of the amount their federal tax return indicated to be due.

> "The two of us are Christians who are seeking to live
> according to the way of Jesus. Our allegiance to this Way
> takes priority over other claims including those of the political

state in which we live. Historically, most of the Mennonite people of whom we are a part have been unable to obey commands of the state regarding participation in war and violence because the Way of Jesus teaches love and concern for all persons, including the 'enemy.' We reaffirm our commitment to this Way of love for the 'enemy.'

"The question whether our commitments to the way of Jesus allow us to support warfare through the payment of the military portion of the income tax has become an urgent one for us. As conscientious objectors to war, we can no longer justify our own subsidizing of the machinery of death which our country creates and controls. We can no longer be content to accept our government's recognition of our moral scruples against personal participation in war at the price of our dutiful subsidizing of the participation of others through military taxes.

"We are deeply offended by the policies governing the distribution and use of American war machinery, particularly in the third world. During our five-year residency in East Jerusalem and Beirut (1971-1976), we were frequently appalled by the destructiveness of the use and very presence of arms from our country. We remain morally offended by American complicity in the arming of both sides in the Middle East conflict to an extent that endangers the entire world. We have reached the point where our values as followers of the Christ no longer allow us to contribute to this abuse of human beings; we find ourselves subject to a law which is higher than that of the state."

The second example of civil disobedience involved their son, Todd. When he reached his 18th birthday in 1981, Todd, like Jacob Wiens, deliberately failed to register with the federal government's conscription system. Todd spoke publicly about his refusal and was supported in that regard by his family and congregation. The local daily paper published an op-ed in which Todd explained his decision:

"Registration is our government's subtle way to prepare us for the growing militarization of our society. One writer compares it to a train. Its destination is nothing other than war and misery. Should one sign aboard now simply because the train has not yet left the station, comforting one's conscience with the thought that there will always be another chance to jump? Even if that were so, how would we explain to ourselves that we did nothing to warn the other passengers?"

. . . . .

"I am deeply concerned by the growing militarization of our society as evidenced by the return of registration, talk of a draft in the near future and an ever-increasing budget for the Pentagon. As a result, rather than fleeing to another country, I have chosen to stay in my community and bear the consequences of my decision."[5]

At Christmas that year (1982), we brothers and our families gathered at Mom's house in Mountain Lake. During our time together we talked with Todd about what he would do if the federal government came after him. Todd, just back from a study term in China, asked us for advice about what he should do next.

I asked whether he viewed nonregistration as an act of obedience to God or, on the other hand, an act of witness against evil. Todd seemed puzzled by my question. Being a witness is an act of obedience, isn't it? Yes, it can be, I said. But many forms of witness involve elements of judgment and choice. Did he consider registration to be sin because it would imply endorsement of a system we should oppose? Perhaps, Todd replied, especially in light of our society's worsening addiction to militarism. But he wasn't sure.

In late February, Federal Bureau of Investigation agents showed up as Todd's door with questions. The U.S. attorney put Todd on notice that a criminal prosecution was being prepared.

In early March, Todd registered. He had begun to doubt his motives, wondering if his resistance was "a quixotic attempt at moral purity." As he wrote in the Goshen College newspaper, he re-read the registration form and "realized I no longer had any trouble filling it out."[6]

For my part, I have been left to wonder if my counsel to Todd reflected a false distinction between obedience and witness. Yes, we function daily within a moral hierarchy of cause and effect. The closer the connection between my actions and a resulting effect, and the more able I am to avoid that effect by adjusting my actions, the more culpable I am if harm actually occurs. When between my act and a harmful effect are a series of independent decisions made by others, then I do not bear responsibility for the harm.

Yet for people of faith, such an analysis is only the first step. Still ahead are questions of witness and integrity. Thus, several Mennonite groups took strong stands against the purchase of war bonds during the early 1940s. The U.S. government explicitly marketed those bonds as a way to support participation in World War II; buying a bond under such circumstances communicated support for the war effort.

All of these same considerations come into play when considering tax resistance. No, we are not morally culpable for each and every wrong committed by the government with our tax dollars. On the other hand, the particulars of the tax and/or the conduct of the government may change the moral calculus. And so we are led into a conversation that is more political than religious, more about interpreting the times and seasons than citing chapter and verse from the Bible. Given what is happening in the broader environment in which we live and the impact those events are having on people and society, are public acts of dissent required?[7]

There are no bright lines here. And that's okay; what is important is to be part of a community that actively and honestly engages such questions.

Dissent in the Workplace

My experience as a public dissenter began in the early 1980s. Along with other members of the Faith Mennonite Church in Minneapolis, I regularly participated in a vigil at the headquarters of Honeywell, a prominent and influential Minneapolis corporation that established its reputation making thermostats and then moved much of its work into research and manufacture for the U.S. military. We picketed other arms manufacturers in the Twin Cities area too, trying to let the public know how these companies were contributing to the arming of the world.

Sharon and I also joined worship services and marches organized by Roman Catholics to express solidarity with the victims of violence in Central America and to protest U.S. government support for those committing that violence.

I understood the legal work I did in those years to be a mild form of dissent, even though it all occurred within conventional norms and channels. It made the power of the law available to the powerless, helping them to gain access to resources otherwise unavailable to them.

None of these activities required unusual courage and maybe they didn't even qualify as dissent. They put us in contact with like-minded people, provided access to information we would not have otherwise received, and lifted our spirits. In general, this sort of activism enriched our lives.

Often more challenging and risky is dissent that occurs inside an organization where one works. At least that was my experience during the 1990s when I worked at Mennonite Central Committee.

Throughout that decade, various parts of MCC embraced an internal action plan to dismantle institutional racism. Called Damascus Road, it included a very broad definition of racism ("power plus prejudice") and a very broad exemption for people of color ("they have no power and thus cannot be racist"). This core analysis led inexorably to the conclusion that nearly everything in the largely white MCC system was racist. Though this approach had the taste of castor oil, most MCCers stoically swallowed it, considering it to be part of the price of being progressive Mennonites.

I didn't like it and said so in various work-related settings. In general, Damascus Road struck me as disingenuous and unlikely to lead to healthy and productive diversity. By rehearsing racial injustices and labeling as racial what often were more truly cultural and economic differences, I said we would widen the perceived distance between people of different racial backgrounds and heighten what was already a legitimate sense of grievance. And by a narrow focus on titular power and official roles, we would end up reinforcing hierarchical aspects of organizational life. I feared Damascus Road would cause us to focus inward rather than outward and create a culture where staff jockeyed for power while mouthing scripted and politically correct talking points. If that happened, relationships and the mission out there in the real world would suffer.

In my view, MCC had an alternative: pay more attention to constituent congregations that had African-American and Hispanic members and allocate more resources to programs those communities found effective. While I led the U.S. Service Program, we reprioritized funds to do just that: a local voluntary service program that served local congregations in at-risk neighborhoods.

But Damascus Road went forward and, as I had feared, focused huge amounts of staff and board time on shifting power inside the organization and changing the complexion of MCC's staff. I supported affirmative hiring procedures but thought program reform should drive the dynamic. If the program responded to the crisis in many of the communities of color where there were active Mennonite congregations, then so would the hiring practices of the organization. In the end, I lost not only the argument but also the regard of some of my colleagues.

Only time will tell who was closer to the mark on this. Certainly good work has been done at MCC and throughout the broader church by participants in the antiracism effort. Just as certainly, there are other ways this agenda could have been pursued to achieve positive results.

Patriarchy also received a lot of attention at MCC during the 1990s and I again found myself holding a minority view. To my way of thinking, patriarchy described a general form of social organization and was not in and of itself a moral wrong. Before people could renounce that way of organizing family and social life in a particular place and time, they would need to know more about how it was implemented. In other words, patriarchy could be good or it can be bad, depending on what it did to women, children, and men.

I fully supported efforts to increase the number of women in leadership positions. That goal was not controversial within any part of MCC, even among the more conservative groups. Yet many of MCC's supporting constituencies, especially the Old Order groups, followed patriarchal family patterns. It seemed a bit dishonest to denounce their social patterns while actively soliciting their financial resources.

The initiatives to root out racism and patriarchy both were organizing campaigns aimed at changing MCC from the inside out. This required first that the legitimacy of existing authority structures and leaders be cast into doubt. To animate this core strategy, both initiatives employed periodic training sessions, some a week long, where staff were invited to recognize the complicity of our employer in the sins of race and gender-based power. We then were invited to become members of action teams that would move the organization toward transformation. As one might expect, my boss wasn't enthusiastic about these trainings; he usually sent me rather than attending himself. And so I participated, often dissenting but searching for some common ground.

I describe these examples of workplace conflict not because I am sure of the correctness of my positions but to make the point that dissent is relevant to many contexts, not just those related to government.[8] What qualifies an action as dissent is that it is public, it addresses matters of broader concern, and it gives voice to views that are disfavored. It is necessary whenever laws, social conventions, or plausibility structures block candor and the speaking of truth.

And when dissenting, there is always the possibility that the reason one's views are disfavored is that they are wrong.

Illegitimate Authority

Because so many Anabaptists in 16th century Europe died for their faith, we remember them as dissenters. As we reflect on the role of dissent in our own lives, it is important to delve a bit deeper into the implications of their experience.

In that time and place, authority had been centralized in the sovereign and the church hierarchy. Each supported the other's legitimacy; that is, the church buttressed the sovereign's exclusive claim to govern with the blessing of God, and the sovereign enforced the church's exclusive claim to know the truth about God. In this power-sharing relationship, the sovereign wielded this world's raw power (swords and soldiers) while the church wielded power over people's destination in the next world (hell or heaven).

Martin Luther and other leading reformers called for changes in the Roman Catholic Church and then eventually, for a new church entirely. Yet they generally showed continued respect for the two-headed authority structure. They simply wanted to replace the Roman Catholic Church with another, reformed church.

In response to these dynamics, the Anabaptists acted primarily with religious motives. They studied the Bible together and came to believe that through the work of the Holy Spirit and the fellowship of those who followed the way of Jesus, God's grace was available to common people without the mediating role of the church hierarchy. Thus, they no longer believed the Roman Catholic Church (or the hierarchies that replaced it in some places) had the authority to condemn people to hell. Nor did it have the authority to bestow divine legitimacy on kings, queens and princes.

If the sovereign's use of power was arguably illegitimate, then disobedience to the king did not amount to disobedience to God. So while the Anabaptists continued to fear the king's sword, they no longer feared eternal damnation beyond the grave. Some directly applied these new beliefs to political life (Zijbrandt Claesz, introduced in Chapter 1, is an example), but most focused instead on bringing the ordinary aspects of daily life into conformity with their understanding of the Bible.

In our time, the slogan "the personal is political" reminds us that choices we make in our private lives can contribute to broader social change and thereby transform the political landscape as well. The refusal of the Anabaptists to baptize their infant children, and their practice of rebaptizing adult believers who desired membership in local congregations, are examples of this. These personal acts communicated dissent from the claims of the state church. This in turn eroded the legitimacy of secular rulers who depended on the state church to sanctify the state's use of the sword.

This is why Charles V, Emperor of the Holy Roman Empire, and his minions reacted to the Anabaptists with such ferocious violence. Without the legitimacy conferred by God via the state church, they believed secular authority would erode and social order would disintegrate. So they felt justified when killing the Anabaptists.

In our time, their story has been used in ways that may suit our preferences but are not faithful to their experience. As noted above, most Anabaptists did not pursue overtly political goals. Thus, we can not claim they were politically active in our contemporary sense. Rather, by paying primary attention to the faithfulness and integrity of their lives, they contributed to the broader political changes that followed.

And while they challenged the exclusive claims of state churches to dispense God's grace, they did not go so far as to say we can fully experience this grace as individuals without the guidance and support of a group that holds authority in our lives. (In part, this is the point of Chapter 3.) Nor did they believe that because of God's grace, all will be well in the end for all of us, no matter how we conduct our lives. These are embellishments we add to their story in an effort to justify our liberal preferences. But they don't really fit.

Yet I do think their example provides guidance for us in our political context. When they refused to join the pretense about the unity of God's will and the state's decrees, the façade of legitimacy began to crack, revealing the raw greed and power-seeking beneath. This revealing served to leash the authority of the state. George Orwell described the dynamic when he said, "During times of universal deceit, telling the truth becomes a revolutionary act."

This brings us to our current situation. We no longer have governments that claim to act for God and condemn us to hell when we deviate from their pronouncements. But as in the 16th century, our governments employ deception to legitimize their overreaching[9]. The story of the Anabaptists encourages us to separate ourselves publicly from this deceit, and then to let the chips fall where they may.

Since August 2006, I've been trying to find my way in what strikes me as an analogous context. That's when I read a book by an eminent theologian, David Ray Griffin,[10] who says we have not been told the truth about the terrorist attacks of September 11, 2001. It jolted me like a slap to the face, a kick to the gut. In the course of my reading, I became convinced the official conspiracy theory advanced by the U.S. government and by the mainstream media is false, and that yet-unnamed individuals within the U.S. enabled the events of that awful day to occur.

During my lifetime, assassins took the lives of John F. Kennedy, Martin Luther King, and Robert Kennedy. Many lies and many unanswered questions have swirled around each of those killings.[11] For the most part, I have paid little attention because I've not perceived those events or their consequences to reach and threaten the things I find most important in life.

But because of the formative power of the official 9/11 conspiracy theory, this is different. The deception has become a core support for the legitimacy of the U.S. military's projection of force around the world to dominate other peoples. Each time a president wants the support of the American people for the exercise of imperialism, he reverts to 9/11 as the core rationale. Each time politicians talk about America's role in the world, they bring it up. Their messages, linked as they are to images we carry in our memories, powerfully shape our perception of ourselves within the wider world. Even in my congregation, as we reflect on living our faith, people often assume we are under constant threat of attack by those who hate our way of life.

Yet we still do not have an explanation of what happened on 9/11 that will withstand close examination. Indeed, it is more likely than not that at least parts of the attack were planned and executed by agents of the U.S. government.

In response to all of this, I have spoken to people in my family and congregation and corresponded with a variety of Mennonite leaders. I've submitted a half-dozen letters on the subject to national Mennonite publications and another dozen to my local Lancaster newspaper. My purpose has been to challenge the fear engendered by this false narrative and delegitimize the war and militarism the U.S. government has pursued in its name. By voicing my views in public, I also hope to find comrades who will discern with me how we can exorcise the power of the 9/11 deception.

My willingness to raise the 9/11 issue seems to have changed people's perception of me. The reigning consensus among leaders and opinion-shapers in my community and across this country is that discussion of alternative explanations of 9/11 is out-of-bounds. Not illegal, but socially taboo. The mainstream media won't touch it; those who come forward with information contradicting the official conspiracy theory are ignored and isolated. It is the most remarkable display of social power I've experienced in my life and is entirely informally mediated and enforced. Those who violate this taboo are marginalized; they have demonstrated poor judgment and an inability or unwillingness to function within social norms. For this they must pay a price.

Such consequences often accompany dissent. And while it's important to count the cost, it also is important to assess what is at stake if we fail to dissent: our descendants' understanding of themselves and the world will be distorted by a lie and they are more apt to lend their support to yet more violence inflicted by the U.S.A. and its government.

*****

During the 2008 presidential campaign, I attended two Obama campaign rallies in Lancaster where he spoke. And I voted for him in the general election, the first in my life in which my vote added to the winner's tally. But I didn't take an active part in the campaigning, even though many friends and relatives actively campaigned and even though I was surrounded by political activism at my office in the Pennsylvania headquarters of the Service Employees International Union.

I took a pass on campaign work because of what I had learned about the attacks on the American people on September 11, 2001. Obama clearly had no intention of re-opening the investigation of that day; that meant it would be business as usual in America. Deciding which candidate would more effectively marshal the pretense of empire no longer seemed important. In November, after Obama's victory, I wrote the following poem.

Preparing Ourselves for a President

Oswald didn't fire the bullets
that remind our leaders
to wield their powers with great care.
He was standing at the entrance
of the school book depository,
watching like the rest.

"I'm just a patsy," he told the world,
someone fixed to take the blame,
then die on national TV.
Though the facts were on his side,
we had more important things to do
than insist justice have its day.

Blaming Oswald became our ritual,
the Kool-Aid we sipped
as we rose up through the ranks.
It conveyed sophistication
to disdain conspiracy
and not go digging in the muck.

So no surprise when our new leader,
who sparks our hopes and
emboldens our dreams,
says he'll hunt the dead bin Laden
and treat official crimes
with benign neglect.

This is how he shows he's ready
to wield the power
and look under the rug.
And we, party to ambition's bargain,
celebrate his wit and steady grace
mourning the mettle we have lost.

*****

During the summer of 2009, Mennonite Church USA hosted a national delegate assembly. One of the items on the delegates' agenda was discussion of our identity as Mennonite Christians living in the most powerful nation on earth. I tried to add intensity and focus to the delegates' preparation for that discussion. In addition to lots of emails, I penned a letter, published by my church's national publication, that included these words.

> "While every government is fallen, the one over us has embraced deceit and violence. It has jumped the tracks and is running amok. We saw this with the illegal invasion of Iraq. We see it again now in the expansion of war in Afghanistan and the daily bombings in Pakistan. And we will see it far into the future through a steady diet of government propaganda that makes the American people afraid and then offers violence as our savior."[12]

To my dismay, little agenda time was made available by Mennonite Church USA leaders for the delegates to speak in open session about the crisis we face as a church within the empire. I do not know why that decision was made. Certainly in many church circles, debate around the implications of empire is not welcome because it is divisive and can undermine the financial health of church institutions. This is a significant consideration, to be sure.

Nevertheless, what we need even more than financially strong church institutions is a "confessing church" such as Dietrich Bonhoeffer helped lead in Germany during the 1930s. It is a church that proclaims allegiance to Jesus Christ, disavows U.S. efforts to dominate the world, dissents from the fear-mongering by our leaders, and begins to free us from falsehoods that have captivated our minds. It is a church that encourages its members to be creative in finding ways to stand apart from the imperial agenda while staying in relationship with neighbors.

This is an urgent matter. Do we imagine we have the strength to ignore the propaganda that surrounds us? Do we imagine we can ingest a daily diet of lies about terrorism and American exceptionalism without losing our way? Not unless we regularly are detoxified, led to repentance, and renewed in hope by a dissenting community.

This is not about whether the U.S. empire is better or worse than empires before it, or whether our life here in America is more or less comfortable than it would be were we living under some other government. Nor is this about coming up with a way to fix our broken political system, or securing our escape from the disastrous consequences of the choices U.S. leaders have made in recent years.

The heart of the matter is this: that we retain the capacity to see the world as it is, the deep desire for it to be renewed, and the courage to participate in God's saving acts, which most certainly will continue long after the current powers collapse. By making peace with the pervasive deception that has come to characterize American life, we close ourselves off to these life-giving qualities. That is what is at stake in this time, living in this place. That is why we need to put distance between ourselves and the powers over us, and again become a confessing church.

Elijah and the Prophets

What if there's no other life
where the crooked is made straight?
If this the life that counts
what may we hope for come tomorrow?

Only conviction, dissent,
and the power of example.
The proof of the pudding
will be in the eating.

Like Elijah and the prophets of Baal,
each will insist, "My lord is god."
Those that believe will follow;
those that don't, won't.

And if we follow,
and if our Lord is God,
then the earth will be blessed;
the people will see the Light.

---

[1] Augustine of Hippo, source unknown. He lived in North Africa 354-430.

[2] Plett, Delbert F. *Saints and Sinners – The Kleine Gemeinde in Imperial Russia,* Crossway Publications, 1999, at 96-97, 128-129.

[3] Quoted in Plett, *Saints and Sinners – The Kleine Gemeinde in Imperial Russia,* at 275.

[4] LeRoy's and Carol Nickel's children are Todd, Chad and Tiffany.

[5] Friesen, Todd. *South Bend Tribune,* March 31, 1982 at 13.

[6] Friesen, Todd. *The Record,* March 11, 1983 at 3.

[7] In April, 2010, Sharon and I for the first time failed to pay the full amount required by IRS Form 1040 (the federal income tax return). In a

letter to the IRS Commissioner, we explained that the U.S. government "has become a threat to peace in the world" and that "a future court may find that in the illegal invasions of Iraq and Afghanistan, the conduct of those wars, and the treatment of prisoners held in U.S. custody, U.S. officials have committed war crimes prohibited by international law." The letter goes on to state: "As Christians and followers of Jesus Christ, our conscience convicts us in these matters and finds us guilty of supporting with our money what we would never support personally, Paying people to kill people cannot be an innocent action."

[8] Yoder, John H. "Mennonite Political Conservatism: Paradox or Contradiction" in *Mennonite Images: Historical, Cultural and Literary Essays Dealing with Mennonite Issues*, Hyperion Press Limited, 1980.

Yoder wrote: "But the disciples of the Lord Christ are not limited to a position they take toward what Caesar is doing. They themselves are building a kingdom. They themselves are creating structures which are alternatives to what has gone before; not in the sense of leaving the world behind or smashing it, but as projecting alternatives, testing pilot models of how any society might be structured. Instead of saying simply 'yes' or 'no' to Caesar's lordship, the church (like the synagogue before her) creates by her very presence the beginning of a permeable, polycentric, pluralistic society." Id., at 12-13.

[9] William Stringfellow described this overreaching as a manifestation of the state's delusion that it is "sovereign in history" and "the power in relation to which the moral significance of everything and everyone else is determined." It is America's "lust to be the holy nation" that prompted him to call it "the Antichrist." See Stringfellow, William. *An Ethic for Christians and Other Aliens in a Strange Land,* Wipf & Stock Publishers, 1973 at 51, 113-4.

[10] Griffin, David Ray. *Christian Faith and the Truth Behind 9/11: A Call to Reflection and Action,* Westminster John Knox Press, 2006.

[11] The many unresolved questions related to the murder of President John F. Kennedy are explored by James W. Douglass in *JFK and the Unspeakable,* Orbis Books, 2008. Douglass also recounts Kennedy's transformation as president into a peacemaker and his efforts along with Nikita Khrushchev's to avoid nuclear war and counter the pursuit by their own military commanders of world dominance.

[12] *The Mennonite*, Mennonite Church USA, June 16, 2009 at 4.

"Set your mind on God's kingdom and his justice
before anything else
and all the rest will come to you as well."[1]
Jesus of Nazareth

Chapter 5: What story do we live by?

Whatever era we live in, we live by a story. It's not a choice; it's simply the way humans are. Always, except in rare times of utter confusion, there is some meta-narrative in our minds giving coherence to the way we conduct ourselves. That's the story we believe in, even if we are not religious.

The story we embrace provides a context for our living and supports the path we have chosen. It helps us to make sense of what otherwise would be an overwhelmingly complex and often baffling existence. It organizes like-minded people into social networks so we can interact with a relatively high degree of confidence. It enables us to cope with our anxiety about death and to channel the subconscious energy that anxiety generates into productive purposes.

The story our ancestors lived by was religious. It described what God had done in the world in Jesus Christ and how God wanted them to live. And it enabled them to embody communally an alternative political reality that spoke volumes to neighbors and friends, kings and princes. They did this despite opposition that occasionally caused disruptions and dislocations, even death.

Why did the story they believed have such power?

Were our ancestors able to answer, they likely would say the power of the story lay in its truthfulness. That's why they were so willing to sacrifice: the narrative had been authored by God. They may have gone on to add that eventually, the truth of the story would be revealed for all to see, if not in this life, then in the life to come.

Such an answer is hard for us to accept because we seldom talk of "truth," may doubt that God wrote the Bible, and may question whether there is a life to come. Is there an explanation for the power of the story they lived by that is more intelligible, and more relevant, to us in our time? This chapter will attempt to provide that.

This reflection will be most useful if we also consider our own lives. What story do we live by? Is it life-giving and empowering? Does it give us the courage and strength to unite with others in support of what is just and right?

Our First Story

Sharon and I were raised to live by the Christian story. But it was a different version than the one our more distant ancestors lived by. Here is the story Sharon and I were taught as children.

As God made the world in the beginning, it was a place of harmony, beauty and fruitfulness. But men and women in their pride disobeyed God. This led to chaos and violence.

God responded by launching a recovery project among the ancient Hebrews, a weak, unorganized slave people living in Egypt. God freed them from the Egyptians, gave them the land of Palestine, and asked them to be a holy people bearing witness to God by living according to God's law.

By "bearing witness", God meant for the people of Israel to be a light to the nations, pointing them to the true God. In the words of *Isaiah*, the people were to do this by creating a place where no child would die in infancy and no old men would fail to live out their years; where people would build houses and live in them, plant vineyards and eat their fruit; where everyone would enjoy the fruit of their own labors and no one would toil for others; where no parent would raise children for misfortune and no one would cause hurt or harm to others.

This initiative on God's part led naturally to the sort of political dynamics we read about in the Hebrew scriptures. Among the Hebrew people, prophets and kings contended with each other around whose version of the truth was an accurate reflection of who God is. Among the nations, Israel contended with its neighbors for the autonomy to live out its understanding of God's way for humankind.

But this attempt to reverse the impact of sin and disobedience failed because of the forgetfulness and rebelliousness of the Jews. So God abandoned this approach and turned instead to changing the hearts of individuals, one at a time.

In this second plan, God used one feature of the first: a Messiah, or deliverer, living among the Jews and embodying God for all to see. This Messiah – Jesus – is the new light to the world. But as reconfigured in this second plan, the Messiah doesn't lead the Jews and other peoples to a restored creation. Instead, he invites individuals to open their hearts to the transforming presence of God's Spirit and thereby prepare themselves for an eternal home in heaven.

In other words, God has abandoned save-the-world politics and instead embraced save-the-soul religion.

In this new era of human history, God's Spirit invites each individual to make a personal commitment to Jesus Christ. Those who accept this invitation know the immediate joy of God's presence and enjoy eternal life with God in heaven. Those who do not accept the invitation struggle on under the burden of sin and face only more suffering in the next life.

In summary, from the Old Testament to the New Testament, individual human beings moved to the center of the cosmic drama. What will I decide? What will you decide? We each are like Jacob of old, wrestling with God in a drama that will seal our fates.

Both Sharon and I decided at a very young age that we wanted to be with Jesus in heaven. My decision occurred at age four during an evening devotional in which my mother talked about a particularly vicious tornado that had devastated a neighboring community. I recall my decision elicited happiness from my family and made my heart sing. Sharon's decision occurred when she was eight or nine. She requested her mother's help in "accepting Jesus" and her mother prayed with her, after leading her through the text of *John* 3:16: "God loved the world so much that he gave his only Son, that everyone who has faith in him may not die but have eternal life."

*****

There are several serious problems with this version of the story.

One is the questions it raises about a Creator God who changed the plan of salvation midway through recorded history. Doesn't this suggest God is unreliable? In my youth, this problem was easily dismissed: God knew all along a change in plans would be needed because of the stubbornness and disobedience of the Jews. So the first plan of salvation was merely preparation for the second. But might God's second plan of salvation be mere preparation for yet a third? This was never asked.

A second and related problem concerns what to do with the Hebrew scriptures (what we called the Old Testament). The broader church has always insisted the Hebrew scriptures are the word of God and remain authoritative for our lives. Thus, we Christians have continued to read the Old Testament, praying our way through *The Psalms* and puzzling our way through the prophets. The highly political context of these writings, and the many references to "the nations," has been especially baffling. In light of God's new plan of salvation, how is David, the shepherd boy who became a guerilla fighter and then a king caught up in a swirl of palace intrigues, a paradigm for our lives?

During my lifetime, this second problem has been "solved" primarily by connecting the political themes of the Old Testament to the modern state of Israel. Thus, the promises God made to Abraham and the Jewish people have been passed to that particular regime. One might imagine Jews as an ethnic group, or the people across the world who faithfully practice Judaism, would be the contemporary beneficiaries of the covenants of God. But instead, the story as I learned it focused on a particular state called Israel and God's faithfulness in blessing the exercise of power by its government. In short, the First Testament was transformed into a propaganda tool for Zionism.

The third problem with the story as we learned it has to do with the disabling fear it elicits among some who believe it. All of eternity depends on the authenticity of a decision we make during a private wrestling match with God. Were we genuine when we said "yes"? Was our confession of sin sincere? Has God, who knows our every motive and every reservation, written our name in the book of life, thus documenting our soul will enjoy eternal bliss rather than suffering?

These unanswerable questions created a stressful dynamic in which many of us found ourselves at risk of being doomed because we failed to get the emotions of our conversion experience just right. In the lives of many people, this played itself out through repeated conversion experiences, frequent re-committals, and self-doubt.

Great-grandfather Gerhard Friesen was baptized as a young man in Nebraska, probably by his Uncle Abraham, the elder of the *Kleine Gemeinde* congregations. This baptism was omitted from the obituary written by my great-grandmother. Instead, she wrote:

> "He often said that the Holy Spirit worked and made him realize his lost condition. So in faith in God he turned to Him and received forgiveness of his sins He was baptized upon confession of his faith [at age 54] and received into the [Holdeman Mennonite] Church at Montezuma, Kansas."

My grandfather Friesen also was baptized as a young man by the *Kleine Gemeinde* congregation in which he had been raised. After marriage, he and my grandmother attended a somewhat more pietistic Mennonite congregation for nearly 25 years. When my teenaged father was baptized by a Mennonite Brethren congregation, Grandpa joined him and at age 48 was baptized a second time. At age 56, while living in Mountain Lake, he responded to an alter call from an evangelist and received yet again his longed-for "assurance of salvation."

Aunt Marcella was baptized by the Carson Mennonite Brethren Church as a teenager. Later, she attended Moody Bible Institute, graduated from Tabor College, and served as a Mennonite missionary in the Congo. She describes the ordeal of trying to confirm her salvation as emotionally harrowing. As a girl, she recalls coming home to an unexpectedly empty house and concluding that while she had been away, Jesus had raptured her parents to heaven, leaving her behind for condemnation. Until her parents arrived home a few hours later, she was terrified and filled with despair. In her early thirties, Aunt Marci abandoned the Christian story completely. She reports her life has been happier and more peaceful as a result.

I didn't personally experience the sort of anguish she experienced; apparently my conversion at age four convinced me I was in the clear. But both my parents struggled with doubt as well. Here is Mom's account of such an experience at about age 25 years.

> "On the Redding farm, I had an experience with the Lord that made a difference in my life. I had doubts about my salvation, even nightmares. Some days I was so depressed about it I knew I couldn't be a good wife and mother. I had read the Bible and prayed about it. One day when I was getting feed for the chickens from the feed house, I stood there in the mash bin, prayed out loud to God, asked Him to show me some way that I was his child. I couldn't stand the fear and doubt I was

> living under; [I wanted God to] have my life and I wanted His peace. God did meet me there and I went out of that feed house knowing a little more about faith and trusting God. His word had more meaning. I clung to *John* 1:12, my salvation verse at age fifteen: 'He gave the power to become' were the key words for me. I had many conflicts since then, but the assurance bit was settled there. John had a similar experience earlier and I remember how he wept as we prayed about it together and God answered with peace of heart."

Looking back at all of this, I am convinced something was deeply flawed about this version of the story, which became ascendant within our family during the past 150-200 years. It was too much about us and not enough about God, too much about souls and not enough about this world, too much about fear and not enough about courage.

When we look back even further, to our ancestors in the 16th, 17th and 18th centuries, we find a different emphasis. We will turn to that in a subsequent section.

*****

But first, perhaps what is most on the mind of readers is another direction, away from living by any story at all. Before considering another version of the Christian story, perhaps it is useful to discuss the possibility I rejected at the beginning this chapter: whether we can live autonomously, apart from the unwritten scripts that meta-stories provide.

At the beginning of this chapter, I stated my view that except in the most confusing of times, all of us live by a story. Within our contemporary times, one such narrative does indeed tell us we can be autonomous, free from stories we haven't composed ourselves. This account of the autonomous life has been dominant in western culture during my lifetime. I found it highly attractive when a young man, still in college. As I imagined it then, I would make my way in the world based on my own choices, not following a script written by any tradition or ideology.

Of course, I also wanted to be with Sharon, the girl I grew up with and the love of my life. And I wanted to avoid military service and Vietnam, which awaited me as soon as I finished my four-year college degree. The tradition into which I had been born enabled me to accomplish both of those immediate goals – the first via a wedding and the second via classification as a conscientious objector to military service. So I decided to go that far with the story I had been given; it served my interests.

Not long after, Sharon and I began living in the village of Glengoffe, up in the hills an hour's drive north of Kingston, Jamaica. We were novice teachers scrambling to manage classrooms filled with students, desperately lonely, and without a clue about how to behave appropriately in a culture we didn't understand. We no longer aspired to be autonomous; instead, we wanted and needed dependable guides in the strange and complicated place where we were living.

From the vantage point of that village, we also began to perceive life in the United States differently than before. Yes, it offered many choices, so many that it could successfully pose as an unstory, free of the limits other narratives imposed. Yet most of those choices pointed in the same general direction: build a career, become more affluent, consume more stuff, work still harder, demand more from life, and depend more on trendsetters and pop culture to bring us pleasure. The entire enterprise was sustainable only by grabbing a larger share of the world's resources. Notwithstanding the slick packaging, Sharon and I concluded the unstory was also a meta-narrative with lots of strings attached. So from a distance, we developed our critique.

But we also knew that after we left Jamaica and returned to the U.S., it wouldn't be so easy. We again would find the American lifestyle attractive and would want to achieve success on its terms. To resist, we would need dependable supporters and reliable guides, people who would help us swim against that stream, walk into that wind. We would need community and tradition; yes, we would need a different story to live by than the unstory so attractively marketed the media, pop culture and corporate America.

Those three years of dependence in Jamaica forever tarnished our view of autonomy. It is an illusion. Dependence is not an aberration but the norm, even for young, healthy and well-educated individuals such as we were then. Pretending otherwise is silly, like imagining we're not affected by gravity and can live outside its influence. The key question of life shifted for us during those years; it no longer was how to be free but where to place our trust, who to follow, which story to believe.

In *The Peaceable Kingdom*, Stanley Hauerwas put it this way:

> "My power [as an individual] is relative to the power of my descriptive ability. Yet that very ability is fundamentally a

social skill, for we learn to describe through appropriating the narratives of the communities in which we find ourselves. . . . that is why our freedom is literally carried by a community that sustains us in the habits of self-possession—not the least of which is learning to depend on and trust others."[2]

And when speaking of Christian ethics, Hauerwas wrote this:

"[The] first task is to help us rightly envision the world . . . . We can only act within the world we can envision, and we can envision the world rightly only as we are trained to see. We do not come to see merely by looking, but must develop disciplined skills through initiation into that community that attempts to live faithful to the story of God. Furthermore, we cannot see the world rightly unless we are changed, for as sinners we do not desire to see truthfully."[3]

We find an example of this in the current geo-political context in which we live. The U.S. government has emerged as an aggressor nation, invading Iraq under cover of false pretenses and in violation of international law, occupying Afghanistan and entrenching itself there via numerous military bases, and fomenting strife in Pakistan. It constantly threatens war against Iran. It frequently recalls the terror attacks of September 11, 2001 to justify this belligerent behavior, even though parts of the U.S. government may have been complicit in the deaths that occurred that day. Meanwhile, as it floods the media with reports, accusations, and threats to support its aggressive conduct, it portrays us as victims of violence and itself as our righteous and just protector. Generally, the mainstream media facilitate this fiction. We are surrounded by it and often feel powerless to resist.

How does an individual stand against distortions as massive as these? Only by standing within a community and a tradition can we summon the resources to resist. The Christian story is not the only one that can provide resources sufficient to the task, but it is the one I have found to be sufficiently inspiring, insightful and resilient.

Early Anabaptist Version of the Story

So what version of the Christian story did the early Anabaptists and Mennonites live by? How did it animate and empower them to see the world accurately, reject false descriptions of how the world works, and perform courageous acts of public witness? And why did that story change over the centuries? To address these questions, we turn to three writers, two of whom are ancestors.

Pieter Jansz Twisck was a Mennonite pastor and elder in the Netherlands from 1592 until his death in 1636. (Until around 1609 he called himself simply Pieter Jansz; thereafter he regularly added the name Twisck.) He wrote and published extensively and vigorously defended the teachings of Menno Simons and Dirk Philips, two Mennonite leaders from the preceding generation. His *The Peaceful Kingdom of Christ,* an exposition of the 20th chapter of *The Revelation of John,* was first published as a pamphlet in Dutch 400 years ago. Later it was translated into German for use by the Mennonites in Prussia, Poland and Russia. In the early 20th century, it was published in English and distributed in the United States.[4]

Twisck's purpose in writing his pamphlet was to help readers recognize that despite the suffering and evil in the world, they were living in an era of human history in which God's justice and God's peace are unstoppable. He wanted them to affirm, "This is the time long-awaited by humanity; now it is here!"

In support of this assertion, Twisck reminded his readers that during Jesus' ministry in Galilee and Nazareth, Jesus proclaimed "the Kingdom of God" as an earthly, historical reality. This Kingdom, as described by Jesus, existed among and alongside other kingdoms, including the Roman empire which dominated the world in Jesus' time.

Although Twisck strongly preferred the phrase "Kingdom of God" to the word "millennium," he taught that the two described the same thing: the period of human history when Jesus Christ reigns along with those martyred because of their faith in him.

This Kingdom is an earthly reality but not another dominating power. It has no fixed territory, no trappings of authority, no army. Nevertheless, it is powerful. Twisck illustrated this by reference to the Apostle Paul; as reported by the *Acts of the Apostles*, Paul directly confronted Roman governors and kings with the claims of the Gospel.

More typically, however, it is a kingdom of suffering and humility.

> "When we look upon the kingdoms of this world, the greater the authority the more honor and service the potentate or sovereign may command. In this Kingdom of our Lord,

> however, the power and authority of the Ruler becomes great through suffering, patience and by enduring the offenses and evil entreaties of men. . . . . In this manner also the apostles, as its first counselors, ruled this Kingdom in lowliness and did not ask others to serve them, but they themselves, at all times, served and recognized that God had placed them as the very lowest, as it were, appointed unto death."

Twisck insisted that since the coming of this Kingdom of God, the power of evil has been restrained "so that [Satan] would deceive the nations no more."

> "Now since death was robbed of its power, an angel also could bind Satan and cast him into prison, as our text declares that he had a great chain in his hand, a chain made up of many sacrifices, much blood and many lives, strengthened with the obedience of Christ, yea, with his obedience unto death, by means of which the whole law was fulfilled; and through himself, that is, through Christ, the enmity was destroyed . . . .
>
> "This great chain of the law relating to all the commandments, fulfilled and confirmed through the blood of Jesus Christ and his full and complete propitiation, was now strong enough to bind Satan and cast him into prison, and then could the angel proclaim the everlasting gospel to them that dwell upon the earth, and to all the heathen and kindred and people and tongues."

Although bound, Twisck wrote,

> "Satan will [continue] to assail men and lead them into many temptations, but no one who continues in watching and praying to God and pleading with him shall fall unless . . . . he rejects the commandments of God."

Twisck emphasized that Jesus' launch of his Kingdom fulfilled the hopes of the ancient Hebrews and the Jewish prophets.

> "Holy and God-fearing men, both before and after the giving of the law through Moses, hoped for a time . . . . in which the high and inestimable happiness of the human race should be restored to them in its full measure. Concerning this exalted happiness, and the possession and enjoyment thereof, though it be only as a foretaste, Jesus speaks in plain terms, saying, 'Blessed are your eyes, for they see; and your ears, for they hear; for verily I say unto you, that many prophets and righteous men have desired to see those things which ye see and have not seen them; and to hear those things that ye hear and have not heard them'."[5]

Twisck strongly believed in life after death, and that every man and woman would face a final judgment before God. Yet his pamphlet contained few references to the soul, few to heaven, only one to hell, and none to the so-called rapture of the righteous away from the suffering and troubles of the earth.

Instead, he focused his readers' attention on the time in which they lived. It is a time of hope, he said, because in the era launched by Jesus, evil can no long maintain its grip. Kings and princes still govern in their coercive and manipulative ways and oppression and suffering continue. But evil has lost its deceptive power. The light now shines through the widening cracks in the earthly kingdoms. The future restoration of all things, as envisioned by the Jewish prophets, has been secured.

> "All this is fulfilled in the Kingdom of Jesus Christ, which is the church, from the days of the apostles on until the time when this time shall be fulfilled. . . . This present time, the last days, the days of the gospel dispensation, shall end with the end of the world."

For Christians reading his pamphlet 400 years ago, Twisck did not offer escape from the world's troubles. His description of the Kingdom reflected little of the blissful harmony we have come to expect in modern discussions of the Millennium. Instead, within the ongoing trials of life, among the political struggles between good and evil and all the shades of gray, Twisck called his readers to recognize and bear witness to the decisive victory for justice and righteousness already achieved by Jesus

Christ. His was a call to action, to physically embody the Kingdom's unique way of engaging enemies and defeating evil.

This is the story early Anabaptists and Mennonites said "yes" to.

Pietism's Challenge

Early on, the Anabaptist version of the Christian story was challenged by other Christian traditions, especially the Roman Catholic, Lutheran, and Reformed. These confrontations are well known because they sometimes involved the persecution, torture, and execution of the Anabaptists.

Another, even more dangerous challenge to the Anabaptist version of the Christian story came in a friendlier guise: Pietism. Indeed, unlike the others mentioned, Pietism declared its admiration for Anabaptism. It never organized itself formally as a separate body competing for church members. Instead, it functioned as an informal reform movement that impacted the preaching and teaching of nearly all of the formal Christian traditions, including Lutheranism and Reformism.

In Prussia and Poland, Pietism began having a strong impact on Mennonites during the Napoleonic Wars at the beginning of the 19th century. By mid-century, it was very influential among Mennonites in Russia. It shaped Mennonites in the rest of Europe too. According to historians Cornelius Krahn and Cornelius J. Dyck, "No other single religious movement has had such an impact on the Mennonites in all countries with the exception of the Netherlands as Pietism."[6]

What is Pietism? In contrast to the state churches, which put the emphasis on orthodox doctrine, or Anabaptism, which put the emphasis on discipleship and witness, Pietism put the emphasis on the individual and his/her heartfelt spiritual experience. It called for the inward experience of salvation by each person followed by the personal application of God's grace to daily life. Its style was warm and embracing, open to extemporaneous expressions of joy and gratitude to God. In regard to daily behavior, it focused less on nonviolence and forms of group witness and more on separation from the world in regard to alcohol consumption, forms of entertainment, and scrupulous honesty in business dealings.

Pietistic contributions to Mennonite life included warmer and more expressive worship services, peer support through the sharing of personal experience and prayer, greater openness to neighbors and outsiders through activities such as Sunday schools and youth groups, more emphasis on outreach and missions, and a concern for personal purity through self-discipline.

The influence of Pietism entered Mennonite communities from a variety of sources including Lutheran and Baptist preachers, Christian publishers, Bible schools, and parachurch organizations such as Bible societies. This development was remarkable because Mennonites traditionally had resisted teaching from outside groups.

Abraham W. Friesen, my ancestor who led the conservative *Kleine Gemeinde* congregations in Russia from 1838 to 1847, resisted Pietism. In his 1824 letter to Peter von Riesen, the wealthy brother who lived back in Danzig, Abraham conveyed disapproval of his brother's gift of money to support publishing and teaching by the German Bible Society.

> "Although they go out in the name of Christ, that is to say that they call themselves Christians, and call upon Christ for their salvation, at the same time they carry on bloody wars and judge and condemn each other according to their flesh. They also war with the weapons of the flesh such as imprisonment, beatings, fines and other similar loving punishments. They have also altered the baptism which Christ himself has commanded as a sign of his grace and as the covenant of the penitent who have faith. Yes, those of the imperishable seed, namely, those who are born anew through the Word of God.
>
> "But they baptize those who are impenitent, that is to say, those who continue to live according to the flesh as before, those who live in great splendor and pride, which has never yet been pleasing unto God, and other similar things more, such as the baptism of infants, the swearing of oaths, and the taking of revenge. All of this can be found among the [Bible Society]. This clearly demonstrates to us that they do not have the spirit of Christ and Paul says that he who does not have the spirit of Christ, he is none of his."[7]

Although the Bible Society was explicitly Christian and evangelical in its message and theology, Friesen focused on the fact that its members lived in a way that resembled nonbelievers in regard to the use of violence, the swearing of oaths, the baptism of infants, and the display of wealth. He didn't want Mennonites to be confused by this repackaging of orthodox beliefs with what he perceived to be a worldly lifestyle.

Friesen also opposed the teaching of Millennialism, which often was communicated by preachers and teachers influenced by Pietism. Millennialism is about a future time when, it teaches, Jesus Christ will return to earth to establish his perfect kingdom for one thousand years. A variation of this teaching includes the rapture, when true believers will be rescued from the tribulations of this life and taken away to heaven until Christ makes his final return. Today, this variation goes by the name Dispensationalism.

Friesen articulated his opposition in an 1832 letter in which he responded to a minister from the *Grosse Gemeinde*.

> "You write further that we deal contrary to the commandments of love and that in general we are doing wrong against our fellow men because we so firmly reject the teaching of the thousand year reign. Quite to the contrary, we believe what we do because of our love for our fellowmen and that according to the spirit of the Holy Scriptures it is quite proper that we do so. But should we be in error in this, then would that God might open the eyes of our understanding. We hope this is not the case for this spirit has never been understood in such a way by the nonresistant Christians.
>
> "According to the writings of Menno Simons, the Muensterites also pointed and taught in this manner [about a future Millennium] with great earnestness and they were terribly devastated on account of this teaching and were deemed fit for extermination. Therefore we also delineate against this teaching as something frightful and we do so out of love for our fellowmen, in order that no one from among us would have to fall into doubting and error and think to themselves, 'My Lord will not be coming for quite some time.' Or that they might think to themselves, 'Today is not yet truly the time of this reign of peace.' And consequently, they would commence to eat and to drink and guzzle their fill and to beat each other, as we have so many examples before our eyes today, in the intention that they would only be truly

converted to the thousand year reign after the entire population was living in peace.

"Behold! In order to protect everyone among us against such a teaching we perceive the matter to be terrifying, just as frightful as it actually is in fact. When we are to take the kingdom of peace which was so clearly purchased for us by the blood of Christ over 1,800 years ago, and of which he has appointed us his stewards, and then to remove this kingdom of peace so far distant from us. So many thousands have had to die for this faith and still have to die. I ask of you, where does this leave our faithfulness and stewardship of the mysteries of God?

"I will take no part in such a rejection. I cannot consider myself to be very intelligent but nevertheless, I do have knowledge within my heart that the reign of grace of Christ has already found its commencement and that the time of [Christ's first coming] has brought the gospels to life in great might and clarity."[8]

Here, Friesen's concern was to oppose teaching that shifted his congregations' hope and expectation away from the current time and into the future. He wanted his readers to understand that Jesus Christ reigns now through the spiritual kingdom of his followers; this is our joy and solace, not the hope of some perfect but far-distant world. Friesen and other *Kleine Gemeinde* leaders were able to keep both Pietism and Millennialism out of their congregations but it was an uphill battle; their membership dwindled as many left for other congregations.

Pietism fit the spirit of the 19th and 20th centuries, a time in which individual experience was elevated and the constraints of tradition began falling away. Congregations that embraced the warm and personal emphasis of Pietism grew rapidly, including several that were very influential in shaping our family. Among Sharon's ancestors, the Klassen, Voth, Wiebe, and Rempel families all came out of the Gnadenfeld congregation in Russia, a large, vigorous group that embraced Pietism and spread its teachings to others. Among my ancestors, those who lived upriver along the Vistula began to embrace Pietism already in Poland and carried its style and sensibility to Russia.

This included the Balzers, Funks and Duecks. The Mennonite Brethren Church began in Russia in 1860 as an outgrowth of Pietistic ferment. Certainly by the time our ancestors immigrated to the United States in the mid-1870s, the embrace of Pietism was far along for all except the most conservative of our ancestors, the *Kleine Gemeinde* who settled in Nebraska.

Pietism combined with Millennialism removed the Kingdom of God from Jesus' teachings. It made the gospel into a private matter with implications far into eternity but little current relevance for today's peoples and nations. This partly explains how in the space of one generation, from the first world war to the second, young men from the church of my youth went from fleeing to Canada to enlisting in the army.

The Confession of Sarah Klaassen Balzer

My great, great aunt, Sarah Klaassen Balzer, lived in a farmhouse she and her husband, Heinrich, built west of Rat Lake in Carson Township. Along with all of our other ancestors who settled in Minnesota, Sarah and Heinrich had been members of the *Grosse Gemeinde* in Russia.

In 1898, Sarah's husband died at age 45. Shortly after, Sarah wrote the following account of her life. It was published in the *Zionsbote,* a weekly Mennonite Brethren newspaper. It is a moving account of personal faith tested by suffering and loss. I include it here because it exemplifies the way in which many of our first ancestors in the United States expressed their faith, especially after joining with the Mennonite Brethren.

> "Already from my youth God's Spirit worked in my heart, though I didn't know what it was. My dear mother had taught me to pray and also often told us children that we should not fall asleep without praying, which I tried faithfully to do, but it did not satisfy me. When I was 15, I was sick with my nerves for eight weeks. When I became well again I determined to lead a completely different life, but unfortunately I could not do it, for I tried in my own strength and soon realized that I was doing worse and became aware that I was on the broad way [to destruction]. Besides this, I also had a great fear of being [eternally] lost, and often sought solitary spots and cried

and prayed much, though my frivolous nature did not reveal any of this.

"When I was 19, I also went to [baptismal] classes and it was my heart's earnest desire then to attain salvation; at that time too I cried and prayed much. I memorized #476 from the hymn book and then often prayed its words. . . . I longed to have rest and peace in my heart, for I felt keenly the burden of my sin and I thought once I had received baptism it would be lighter, but it made no difference. At that time nothing was said about the possibility of having our sins forgiven.

"In 1874 I was married but the longing for salvation remained in me. We talked about this with each other but told no one else. In 1876 we migrated to America. After three days of travel, our baby boy died, 10 months old, which was almost unbearable for us. It was pitch dark as he was carried outside. The train stopped for only five minutes (the child was given into strangers' hands for burial). Oh, how painful this was for us. . . . As I struggled with this and begged the dear Savior to send me some comfort from his Word, so I could surrender myself to his will, these words came to me: 'And it came to pass that the beggar died and was carried by the angels into Abraham's bosom' (*Luke* 16:22). Because our child could not be buried, this was a great comfort to me. The Lord really drew us to himself at that time.

"When we first arrived here in Mountain Lake . . . . how dreary everything looked: the grasshoppers had taken everything, and we often promised ourselves, if we could just have food and clothing and a small shelter, we would be contented. The Lord granted us this, that we could soon have a place here also to earn our livelihood, but he did not cease working in our hearts by his Spirit. I always felt within myself that I was too wicked, that for me there was no longer grace. I felt keenly my spiritual lostness; we prayed together much and searched in God's Word; we were also to receive some comfort, for example, where it says: 'A bruised reed I will not break, and a dimly burning wick I will not quench' (*Isaiah* 42:3).

"For a time I had great anxiety and severe temptation when I prayed, could only cry and say the words, 'God, be merciful to me a sinner' (*Luke* 18:13). But suddenly, one day as I was again overtaken by such great fear, it came to me: 'In the world you have fear, but be of great cheer, I have overcome the world' (*John* 16:33). Then I fell down in repentance and shame and thanked the dear Lord, for I felt the burden was gone from my heart. Oh how happy I was at that time, that I could appropriate God's Word like that . . . . A year and a half later my dear husband also received forgiveness through the Word, 'but where sin abounded, grace did much more abound' (*Romans* 5:20).

"Because we read much in God's Word and because salvation was a serious matter to us, we soon also discovered that we should let ourselves be baptized yet. . . . We were buried in Christ's death through baptism [into the Mennonite Brethren Church] on October 29, 1882. As we walked to the water, the song 'Jesus, guide our way' was sung. I was especially struck by the verse: 'Though difficult our way/ Steadfast let us be/ Even in the hardest days/ Firmly, uncomplaining/ For through adversity/ Lies the way to Thee.' Over time, I have learned to understand this more than I understood it then.

"In 1885 misfortune struck us when we were burned out because of lightning; everything burned except the livestock. It was painful for us to stand by, almost naked. We then went along with my [relatives] for the night and since I couldn't sleep at all that night, I got up and went outside and gave free rein to my tears. It was June 20 and quite a cold night and because I was wearing everything I owned, I was filled with worry, but *Matthew* 6:25-26 became a comfort to me, that the heavenly Father would care for us; and he did too, thanks to him for it.

"In 1886 the Lord took all our four children [scarlet fever]. There we were, lonely and forsaken; often we had to ask, 'Why Lord?' But there was nothing to do but yield ourselves to God's will. The Lord sought to draw us nearer to himself and oh, how often he let us feel his presence, blessed hours indeed.

"About five years ago [my husband] got a heart condition and though we employed much medical help, it was all in vain. . . . He was able to be up and do light work until last summer, then he could hardly tolerate any food anymore and was so short of breath; he often said perhaps his end would come suddenly, but I could not believe the Lord would take such a way with me, it seemed impossible. I prayed much about his health and also firmly believed that it was a small thing for the Lord to give my dear husband health, but it turned out differently.

"One week before his home-going [death], he said it seemed urgent to him that he put his affairs in order. I could not comprehend it and said, 'What shall I do with the little children [five of them, with a sixth on the way]? I also do not believe the Lord will take you from us.' Then he said his heart was so afraid when he thought about soon appearing before God's face, it would only be grace if he were saved, for he had nothing to show for himself. Then we knelt and prayed and my dear husband asked especially, that if it was God's will that he depart from here, God would give him the grace to meet him joyfully. After praying he said he felt lighter. . . .

"He was very short of breath; he could no longer sleep at night, nearly always had to sit up. I often got up at night and then found him sitting at the table with the Bible; it distressed me that we could all sleep peacefully and he always had to sit up, but he was so calm. . . . Saturday night to Sunday I was overcome with such fear and my chest hurt me so much that I groaned in prayer: 'Lord, what's the matter, surely I'm not steel or stone that you have to take such a way with me.' I implored the Lord to give me strength to yield to his will. I did not want to add to my dear husband's suffering by not being able to let go of him.

"In the morning he was again very short of breath and said, 'I will suddenly be gone and have not put my house in order.' When he was breathing somewhat easier again, he said: 'Now I have to order my affairs.' Again I could scarcely comprehend it, but he said, 'Mama, we've reached that point.' Only someone who has experienced this understands how I felt. Then I told him my experience of that night and how we had to let go of one another. Then he shared with me his thoughts about what would be best for me and our children. . . He [said] the Savior would have special grace for me and our children . . . . Oh brothers and sisters, I will never forget that Sunday, how heartbreaking and yet blessed it was.

"In the afternoon we read this Word together: 'There remains therefore a rest for the people of God' (*Hebrews* 4:9). Several times he said, 'How blissful a rest it will be, when I am finally able to enter the rest prepared for the children of God.' It seems I still hear him saying it. Then we knelt side-by-side and thanked the dear Savior for all the blessings he had given us together and asked for further help in our situation. It was the last time we bent our knees together. When we rose from prayer, my husband was very happy and said, 'We enjoy heavenly food already here.' I could only cry. He looked at me so kindly and said he loved me very much and felt so relieved that I would let him go if this was God's will.

"Monday morning was very difficult again, he had to sit before the open window. . . . Toward evening he said his spirit already lingered above. His breathing became easier. At 8:30 he asked if it wasn't time to close the day [evening prayers] and immediately began to pray. He prayed so clearly and committed us all to the dear Savior and requested that the entrance through heaven's gate would remain clear and open for him . . . . [we sang a song], then he said, 'Soon, soon, the struggle is finished.' Now he felt so tired and wanted to sleep; we settled him as comfortably as possible in the rocking chair and soon he had sunk into a sweet sleep, a peaceful sleep like he had not had in two months. . . . and because we did not sit up with him, we did not notice when, peacefully, without movement or sound, death broke the bond of marriage."[9]

My Confession

Sarah Klaassen Balzer's remarkable testimony describes an important part of our heritage. That heritage shaped me in myriad ways and often for the good. I will give one example.

Nearly every morning, before I get started with my day, I speak to God out loud. I call it prayer. It's part of the devotional practice my parents taught me and involves Bible reading and silent listening as well as speaking.

Who do I listen to and what do I hear? Apart from the frequent sound of John Michael Talbot's recorded voice singing *The Psalms,* it's always been silent; I've never heard another's voice. I believe God's spirit inhabits the earth, surrounding each of us with her energy and insight and guiding our thoughts. So when I'm "listening", I'm paying attention to my thoughts in recognition that God's spirit may be giving me a nudge. It's a risky business because I have lots of silly ideas and have concocted all manner of nonsense during such times of reflection. I don't want to attribute this to God, of course, and so "listening" must be disciplined by what I've learned from other Christians, from the Bible, and from living.

What do I find useful in Bible reading? It gives me a language with which to describe my life. We all know that language is formative; that is, we don't live a certain way and then put words to it. To some degree, language comes first and shapes what we do. In that sense, Bible-reading shapes what I do and how I act over the long-term.

What do I say to God when I pray? There are no rules. Some of what I say is memorized through repetition; the Lord's Prayer is the best example but other little set pieces are my own compositions and have evolved over time. Gratitude and thanksgiving are a constant element, as are prayers for my loved ones, both family members and friends.

During my prayers, I try to identify what within me is causing anxiety or fear. I name it aloud and tell God it is something I trust God to help me address. Sometimes, I stop and try to imagine this "enemy" as the source of something for my good. I don't always succeed but the exercise places my good and my enemy's good together in a space where creativity and imagination can generate new possibilities.

Prayer is a practice that changes me, bit-by-bit, day-by-day. When I consider my actions and attitudes, there is much I wish were different, much I wish to change. When I remember God's faithfulness, when I commit the day ahead to God, something good finds a toehold within me. It is a spirit more open to those around me, more alert to possibilities yet unknown, more confident we will find our way. From a distance, all of this may be incomprehensible. Up close, one sees it for what it can be: tiny, almost imperceptible steps, moving toward the light.

As spiritually engaging as this pietistic practice is, it also fails us by placing huge parts of life outside the circle of God's salvation. It gives us a rich, but private, religious experience and turns much of the rest over to other powers. It leaves us with a divided life and a faith no longer relevant to areas of wider public concern and need. In the following poem, a reflection on the ritual of Holy Communion (the Eucharist), I allude to this dividedness.

Proclaiming Death

Now proclaim we the death of Jesus
confront again our fear of the foe.
Spilt blood and suffering,
a body cold and torn,
these provoke a flinch and a shudder
yet we bring them to the fore.

Our deaths, all those unlatched trapdoors
through which we'll forsakenly fall,
they, too, we pause to ponder
as his murder we recall.

Odd that our preeminent ritual
turns our thoughts toward such dark gloom.
Do the Savior's lacerations
the rank betrayal by his friends
inspire great courage or resignation
as we walk on toward our ends?

As our leaders plot in secret
another round of shock and awe
does recalling death reveal it
or only veil their scheming raw?

Our remembering is meant to alter
the way we measure up our lives;
death the foe is but a juncture
one defeat on victory's run.
So declares our proclamation:
"the death of our Lord until he comes".[10]

*****

I love the verse in the Bible where it says that because of Jesus Christ, evil can "deceive the nations no more."[11] We've seen the truth of this in our own time with the collapse of the Soviet Union, the loss of legitimacy by oppressive governments in South Africa and Israel, and the exposure of the U.S. government's culpability for the September 11, 2001 terror attacks and the criminal invasion of Iraq. Massive efforts to "deceive the nations" were part of each of these situations. Yet each of those efforts at deception has failed or is coming undone.

In the more sophisticated circles in which many of us move, there is real reluctance to call any story "true" or "false". But sometimes being old-fashioned is an advantage and this surely is such a situation. In my view, the story of Jesus Christ is true and worthy of the allegiance of everyone who walks this earth. On the other hand, some stories are so destructive to people and the earth that we should call them "false" and oppose them. The politics of Jesus teaches us how to do this.

There are many ways to oppose a false account of life, starting with a refusal to accept its description of reality or to conform one's life to its assumptions. The way we live day-by-day is a witness in itself. Conversations with friends, neighbors, and co-workers can be places where we make our allegiance known while challenging false accounts. If we are thoughtful about it, we will have the opportunity to make "bigger" decisions that can reflect the story we live by: where we live, how we make our living, who we join, and when we dissent.

As I write this, a false narrative is much on my mind. It is the story of the United States of America, possessor of at least one-half the military might in the world, but allegedly in great danger because of a handful of *al Qaeda* terrorists in the mountains along the border between

Afghanistan and Pakistan. Here are the words of United States President Barack Obama, spoken to the cadets at West Point Military Academy in December 2009, describing how the United States of America will respond to its opponents.

> "Since the days of Franklin Roosevelt, and the service and sacrifice of our grandparents and great-grandparents, our country has borne a special burden in global affairs. We have spilled American blood in many countries on multiple continents. We have spent our revenue to help others rebuild from rubble and develop their own economies. We have joined with others to develop architecture of institutions -- from the United Nations to NATO to the World Bank -- that provide for the common security and prosperity of human beings.
>
> "We have not always been thanked for these efforts, and we have at times made mistakes. But more than any other nation, the United States of America has underwritten global security for over six decades -- a time that, for all its problems, has seen walls come down, and markets open, and billions lifted from poverty, unparalleled scientific progress and advancing frontiers of human liberty.
>
> "For unlike the great powers of old, we have not sought world domination. Our union was founded in resistance to oppression. We do not seek to occupy other nations. We will not claim another nation's resources or target other peoples because their faith or ethnicity is different from ours. What we have fought for -- what we continue to fight for -- is a better future for our children and grandchildren. And we believe that their lives will be better if other peoples' children and grandchildren can live in freedom and access opportunity.
>
> "As a country, we're not as young -- and perhaps not as innocent -- as we were when Roosevelt was President. Yet we are still heirs to a noble struggle for freedom. And now we must summon all of our might and moral suasion to meet the challenges of a new age. . . . .

> "America -- we are passing through a time of great trial. And the message that we send in the midst of these storms must be clear: that our cause is just, our resolve unwavering. We will go forward with the confidence that right makes might, and with the commitment to forge an America that is safer, a world that is more secure, and a future that represents not the deepest of fears but the highest of hopes."

Where I live, most people believe the story told by President Obama. It describes the world as a dangerous place where the U.S. is a righteous god, spilling its own blood to bring security and prosperity to others. It describes U.S. military force as the great protector, U.S. military occupation of other lands as the path to freedom, U.S. military invasions of other countries as noble endeavors. It calls to mind the sacrifice of Jesus in describing the U.S. role in the world, yet denies any intention to dominate and control the resources of others.

How can this false narrative be accepted by someone who is committed to Jesus as the Messiah? By depoliticizing Jesus' story, shifting his purpose far into the future, and focusing on individuals and the eternal destiny of souls. Once distorted in such a fashion, it never occurs to many people that Jesus' story competes for our allegiance with the story told by Barack Obama; they can not both be true.

Compounding our difficulty with all of this is an apparent contradiction: despite the arrival in Jesus of the Kingdom of God, the disappointments of life and the harm inflicted by evil continue. This isn't how we imagined God's reign would be. Something within us rises in protest; we want justice and we want the suffering to stop. Indeed, the Biblical writers often voiced the same desires. Just read *The Psalms* and the anger expressed there about the wealth and arrogance of the wicked.[12]

The dissonance of it all prompts many to conclude the salvation spoken of in the Bible is metaphysical and meant for another place. For this world, we need other saviors to rescue us. Military leaders, hand-in-hand with politicians and the captains of industry, are happy to fill the role because it brings with it huge benefits in power, prestige and wealth.

Our best teachers, such as Pieter Jansz Twisck, have helped us see that the continued existence of suffering is not so remarkable. What is truly astonishing is the stubborn endurance of compassion, sacrifice, courage, kindness and joy. This is what bears witness to the triumph of our Lord! This is the evidence of our salvation!

Yet day-to-day, we struggle to hold the view that the real story of the world, the one most historically significant, isn't the one we read and hear about each day from the empire's representatives. The following poem reflects my effort to stay focused and resist distraction.

Giving Up Empire for Lent

Play music in the morning
let NPR be quiet for a change.
Enough of their turning the awful
into reasonable-sounding things.

That *New York Times* on the newsstand?
Let it lie 'til it's yellow with age!
They provoked the Iraq invasion
now it's Iran we're supposed to hate.

The suits on the evening news
reporting what "an anonymous source" said?
It's just another inside player
dealing both sides of the game.

Let it all go 'til Easter
part of the purge and cleansing we need
if we're to tell truth from fiction.
If we're ever to believe.

*****

It's not just Pietism and American idolatry that elicit my objections. Sometimes I'm at odds with parts of my congregation's teaching. I'm not militant about these differences; the attitude I seek is expressed this way: "My church tells me this is true; I confess it is difficult to accept."

Perhaps such matters are best kept private. As I look back over the years, some of my doubts have been resolved and usually along the lines of my church's teaching. Why document the ones that still remain?

One reason to do so is that some who read this book are outside the church because of their doubts. If candor prompts them to recognize the church is a more diverse and textured community than their stereotype suggests, then describing my doubts is worth the price. A second reason is that my doubts touch on matters I have been discussing in this chapter: where do we perceive this life and this world to fit in God's purposes?

One of my doubts relates to Christmas. It is the story of the incarnation, of the fullness of God coming to dwell on earth in the long-awaited Messiah. It's a gritty story about taxes, a scandalous pregnancy, childbirth far from the needed support of midwife and family, the rude shelter of an animal shed, dirty shepherds bearing witness, and a jealous king bent on infanticide. Taken as a whole, the story declares God has encountered all the pain this world has to offer and yet chooses to dwell here. Perhaps poetry communicates this best.

Return of the Shepherds

Longing shadows our days,
haunts our prayers, disturbs our sleep.
This pointless scrabble,
tedious search for pastures fresh,
awaits divine deliverance
a new beginning 'mid glory bright.

Here at last! Oh expectation,
the skies are filled with wondrous light.
Now has come our long awaited,
the one who'll all our hopes fulfill.
Come! Make haste, prepare to meet him
in Bethlehem, King David's town.

But we find there just a stable,
tired travelers, an infant's sounds.
If this the start of new creation
if this rude habitat his home
what to make of tiresome hillsides?
How regard our low estate?

Yes, he's come to live among us
to save us here from dreary fate;
sheep and fields, humdrum of living,
are graced and changed by this desire.
Because earth his consuming passion
it for us is heaven-drenched.

Christmas is such a strong affirmation for this world and life itself. I find it difficult to reconcile that message with the church's teaching about Jesus' supernatural conception. Most New Testament writers did not consider it essential. In my view, the church's insistence on this point serves to undermine the good news of Jesus Christ, which is that God, who will not be denied, is committed to saving creation as we know it.

Another of my doubts concerns the commonly-held conceit that an essential part of each human being is immortal. This assumption doesn't have its roots in the Christian faith but has found its way into most churches, including mine. It usually is expressed within the context of a discussion of the afterlife, when it is said each person will consciously reside in a place different from this world in which we live. In light of the incarnation and bodily resurrection of Jesus, which together demonstrate so clearly God's intention to restore what God has created, I respond skeptically to such talk; somehow, it doesn't fit.

In my study of the Bible, I find little evidence the writers shared our notions of heaven and immortality. Yes, the book of *Daniel* introduced the idea of a physical resurrection. Jesus taught the resurrection and was the first to experience it himself. This new creation - life beyond death - became a hope frequently expressed by the writers of the Second Testament. But in their anticipation of this gift, they did not adopt the contemporary view that each human being is destined for an eternal, disembodied existence somewhere apart from this earth.

The Apostle Paul, who wrote of these matters more directly than any other writer in the Bible, seemed to teach that those who reject God "perish" at death;[13] God remembers them no more and thus their consciousness is extinguished. But *The Psalms* tell us God remembers the righteous,[14] which I find to be a wonderful way to describe life eternal. Within God's memory the righteous remain, waiting along with the living for God's final, great act of restoration at the end of time.[15]

When Amber and Emily were children and our family talked about a past event, they would ask: "Were we there with you?" We would reply, "You weren't born yet; you were only a thought in the mind of God." Perhaps this gets at the truth of the matter: before first giving us life, God anticipated our being. In a similar way, God anticipates the being of those who have died but will be renewed in the resurrection.

My point isn't to take a firm position on what happens after we die. Rather, I want to challenge those who shift the focus from this life to something else. The Bible opposes such a shift.[16] This point is made by

N.T. Wright, the Bishop of Durham for the Church of England. In *Surprised by Hope,* Wright states:

> "It was people who believed robustly in the resurrection, not people who compromised and went in for a mere spiritualized survival, who stood up against Caesar in the first centuries of the Christian era. A piety that sees death as the moment of 'going home at last,' the time when we are 'called to God's eternal peace,' has no quarrel with power mongers who want to carve up the world to suit their own ends. Resurrection, by contrast, has always gone with a strong view of God's justice and of God as the good creator. Those twin beliefs give rise not to a meek acquiescence to injustice in the world but to a robust determination to oppose it."[17]

When we understand this life and this world to be what God has blessed by God's presence and salvation, then we can whole-heartedly join Jesus in praying, "Thy Kingdom come on earth as it is in heaven."

Here is a whimsical way of making this same point.

Invested

Recently I learned God owned property
near my house, down the line.
Yes, I knew of God's interest
in the general locality
and that a member of the family
once lived here for a time.

But that individual left,
moved on to another place.
Yet apparently the investment
has never been liquidated;
seems God still regards here
as ideal living space.

This put me in a quandary,
sent me into a real spin.
I'd been planning to sell,

leave the property market
before it crashes
and does me in.

Been paying keen attention
keeping myself in the local loop.
And while ordering my affairs
to prepare for departure,
I've tracked the real estate listings
to learn the inside scoop.

Yet somehow I'd missed the fact
the Big Guy's still invested,
keeps paying the taxes
trimming the shrubs
acting like the future
isn't that contested.

Even heard one report
(far-fetched as it may be):
the family member who'd visited
proclaimed before he left
this neighborhood is solid
into perpetuity!

As you can well imagine
my "For Sale" sign is down.
Been painting all the shutters,
fixing windows, caulking cracks;
since God finds here attractive
I want to stick around.

*****

Through the Kingdom Jesus inaugurated, God continues to save the world. This remains a political struggle, as it was in the stories we read in both testaments of the Bible.

But a lot changed with the coming of Jesus, enough to send the shepherds back to their fields and us back to our routines with a changed understanding of life. We have begun to grasp God's unequivocal and tenacious commitment to creation. We are pulling free of misguided notions of God's Kingdom as another government and God as another war-fighter. In place of such ideas, we now understand the Kingdom as a way of life followed each day by people all over the world, a way of life that pursues reconciliation and restoration rather than separation and annihilation. This way of life has the quiet power to expose deception and dethrone presidents, generals and CEOs, even while it remains vulnerable to the pain and suffering of life.

After all, we already have experienced the acts of God in our own lives. In the words from the Second Testament, while we were still enemies, when we were completely without merit and not deserving of any good thing, God reconciled and restored us and called us good. [18]

Our more distant ancestors believed that with Jesus, God's politics began moving forward with new clarity and vitality. This conviction enabled them to live as courageous nonconformists, not privately in secret faithfulness to God, but in public for the world to see.

Were we to be persecuted as they were, the more pietistic side of our tradition would prompt us to concede to our interrogators, rationalizing our actions by saying, "This is only politics; our concern is eternal life." Throwing ourselves on the mercy of God, we would say whatever our tormenters wanted to hear.

But the martyrs also believed in the mercy of God and in a life to come. Yet many were unwilling to say what their interrogators wanted to hear because they understood themselves to be citizens of the Kingdom, an entity changing the world and bringing hope to people as it bore witness to Jesus Christ.

In the crucible of those interrogations, as the empire's officers demanded they renounce their baptisms, the Kingdom's confrontation with deception and despair reached a decisive moment. Acquiescing to the empire in order to avoid pain would have treated such confrontations as pretend events. To the early Anabaptists, this life was not pretend nor a rehearsal for something else. It was the real deal infused with the drama of citizenship in the Kingdom of God.

A Short Catechism

Q: Who is God?

A: The One who made the world and who is saving it from ruin.

Q: How does God do that?

A: Chiefly through the powerful witness of his son, Jesus the Nazarene.

Q: How can we be part of this?
A: By humbling ourselves, learning to live as he lived, and joining the community of Jesus' disciples.

Q: Then what happens?
A: Our lives become part of the reconciling witness of the Kingdom of God on earth.

Q: How does this all end?
A: The restoration of beauty, justice and harmony in all God created.

Faith in the biblical sense engages the world with the conviction that God is saving it from ruin, and that to participate in the world's restoration is to live in the presence of God. To be in heaven, that is.

Politics in the biblical sense isn't about seizing the power of government to impose one's will on others; instead, it is living an alternative that competes with other stories for the allegiance of our friends and neighbors. Nothing can defeat the Kingdom's politics. But until the end of time, neither will the Kingdom's politics achieve a comprehensive triumph. The struggle will be the journey.

Like those who went ahead of us, let us we prepare wisely and travel with companions who share our understanding of the road ahead. Together, may we live as bravely in our times as they did in theirs.

To Know and Not to Know

Once I thought faith to be right thinking
like learning trig or chemistry.
Not frequently employed but absolutely true
and absolutely necessary
to explain the ways things work.

Sometimes I think of it as a relationship
with a silent partner, trustworthy and strong.
I'm out front keeping busy
but the important stuff happens between us,
quietly and behind the scenes.

Then there's faith as philosophy
a big-picture way of living day-to-day.
It's my hard-earned wisdom
on coping with tragedy
and watching for joy.

These all fall short; none captures the mix
of certainty and the unknown.
For God is mystery who called Jesus "My Son",
life a wacky compass, four points labeled "north".
Faith steps in a direction, imagining it the one He took.

---

[1] *The Gospel According to Matthew,* chapter 6, verse 33.

[2] Hauerwas, Stanley. *Peaceable Kingdom: A Primer in Christian Ethics,* University of Notre Dame Press, 1983, at 42.

[3] Id., at 29-30.

[4] Twisck, Pieter Janz. *The Peaceful Kingdom of Christ,* Mennonite Publishing Company, 1913. Republished in *Storm and Triumph: The Mennonite Kleine Gemeinde 1850-1875,* D.F.P. Publications, 1986, at 311-320.

[5] *The Gospel According to Matthew,* chapter 13, verse 16-17.

[6] Krahn, Cornelius & Cornelius J. Dyck. "Pietism." *Global Anabaptist Mennonite Encyclopedia Online.* 1987.

[7] Quoted in *The Golden Years: The Mennonite Kleine Gemeinde in Russia 1812-1849,* D. F. P. Publications, 1985 at 268-269.

[8] Id., at 255.

[9] Sarah Klaassen Balzer, "A Sister's Experience." *Zionsbote,* September 28, 1898.

[10] *The First Letter of Paul to the Corinthians*, chapter 11, verse 26.

[11] *The Revelation of John,* chapter 20, verse 3. Jesus is quoted in a similar vein by *The Gospel According to Matthew,* chapter 10, verses 26-

27: "So do not be afraid of them. There is nothing covered up that will not be uncovered, nothing hidden that will not be made known. What I say to you in the dark you must repeat in broad daylight; what you hear whispered you must shout from the house-tops."

[12] *The Psalms* speak eloquently to our desire for relief from the suffering caused by oppression. Chapter 73 is but one example.

[13] *The Letter of Paul to the Romans,* chapter 2, verses 1-16. Perhaps Paul is referencing *The Psalms* 73:27 in using the term "perish".

[14] *The Psalms,* chapter 112, verse 6.

[15] *Acts of the Apostles,* chapter 3, verse 21; *Romans* 8:21.

[16] In the first account of Jesus' life and teachings, *The Gospel According to Mark,* we find only two places where Jesus refers to an afterlife (10:30 and 12:24-27) and one where he refers to the annihilation of hell (9:42-48). This simple fact is obscured by the common error of imagining the Kingdom of God, the Kingdom of Heaven, and the coming of the Son of Man as events far into the future, at the end of time. See Douglass, James W. *The Nonviolent Coming of God,* Orbis Books, 1991. According to his first biographer, Jesus' primary concern was the transformation of life before death, not after.

[17] Wright, N.T. *Surprised by Hope,* HarperOne 2008, at 26-27.

[18] *The Letter of Paul to the Romans,* chapter 5, verses 8-10.

Afterword

Over the past few months, while I've been writing, people from my congregation have been making a virtual list of "things you need to know." It's a fun-filled exercise focused on practical aspects of living. As I've become better acquainted with Sharon's and my families' stories, I've found items to include on such a list.

- There are many wonderful places to live; don't cling too tightly to any one of them. Hold your national citizenship lightly and be prepared to give it up when your core identity is at stake.
- Do good work; lots of things qualify.
- Be part of a community, one that speaks truthfully and equips you for the bracing experience of walking into the wind.
- Dissent is part of living in the Kingdom of God.
- Life is important. During times like ours, God's son called this planet home. When we imagine we deserve a better home in another world, we have forgotten his story.

Some of us are looking for help. We feel our environment shaping us into people we never wanted to be: eager to believe lies, glad for the benefits of empire, paying more attention to the performance of our financial investments than the many deaths of innocent people at the hands of our government.

Our families' stories do not presume on our good graces or tell us what we should or must do. They simply remain until we are ready to pay attention, ready to learn what they have to teach. In the words with which I began, "we are free to set sail anytime we want."

*****

Appendix 1: Four Generations before Berry Friesen

Jacob L. Friesen**
(1837-1901)
Maria Enns*
(1837-1855)

Gerhard E. Friesen**
(1862-1930)

Abraham B. Friesen**
(1833-1903)
Helena Kroeker*
(1833-1864)

Helena Friesen**
(1864-1930)

George A. Friesen
(1885-1954)

Heinrich Ratzlaff*
(1820-1864)
Anna Harms**
(1808-1874)

Heinrich T. Ratzlaff**
(1848-1922)

David Flaming^^
(1815-1883)
Maria Lohrentz^
(1818-1873)

Elizabeth Flaming**
(1859-1941)

Elizabeth Ratzlaff
(1883-1948)

John V. Friesen
(1918-1971)

Jacob Wiens**
(1820-1891)
Anna Funk^^
(1820-1904)

Johann Wiens**
(1848-1938)

Abraham Dueck^
(1810-1875)
Maria Dueck*
(1814-1891)

Margaretha Dueck**
(1851-1916)

John J. Wiens
(1885-1950)

Heinrich Baltzer^^
(1820-1896)
Katharina Reimer**
(1824-1901)

Jacob H. Balzer**
(1860-1948)

Bernhard Klaassen**
(1828-1882)
Elisabeth Wiens**
(1827-1881)

Maria Klaassen**
(1860-1907)

Sarah Balzer
(1888-1978)

Blondina Wiens
(1918-1996)

----

^ born in Poland, died in Russia
^^ born in Poland, died in US/Canada
* born in Russia, died in Russia
** born in Russia, died in US/Canada

Appendix 2: Four Generations before Sharon Klassen

Gerhard Klassen^^
(1823-1910) Abraham G. Klassen**
Maria Reimer^^ (1851-1880)
(1825-1905)

Abraham A. Klassen**
______?_______ (1872-1958)
Elizabeth Voth**
______?_______ (1850-1936)

William Klassen
______?_______ (1911-1996)
William Wiebe**
______?_______ (1843- ??)

Justina Wiebe
Jacob Wiens** (1881-1969)
(1817-1897) Justina Wiens**
Justina Dueck** (1848-1922)
(1824-1903)

Daniel Eytzen^
(1784-1845) Johann Eydsen**
Helena Goertzen* (1831-1911)
(1801-1858)

Jacob J. Eytzen**
Franz Janzen* (1860-1941)
Katharina Janzen*
______?_______ (1832-1875)

Esther Eytzen
______?_______ (1915-2009)
Johann A. Wiebe**
______?_______ (1844-1929)

Maria Wiebe**
______?_______ (1871-1949)
Justina Rempel*
______?_______ (1847-1875)

----

^ born in Poland, died in Russia
^^ born in Poland, died in US/Canada
* born in Russia, died in Russia
** born in Russia, died in US/Canada

Appendix 3: Ancestors and Places in Poland

Readers traveling to Poland may appreciate details about places our ancestors lived. Here are such details, most gathered from *Grandma's Window,* California Mennonite Historical Society, 2004. The number after each name indicates the generational distance to Sharon or me.

Berry's Ancestors

Hans Ratzlaff (11) Born around 1590 in Stettin (Szczecin); later lived at Wintersdorf (Przechovka). Believed to have been a soldier in a Swedish campaign in Poland, he converted to the Christian faith, married a Mennonite woman, and left his sword embedded in a fence post. Descendants lived west of Culm (Chelmno) near Schwetz (Swiecie).

Abraham von Riesen (7) Probably from a Prussian family, he married in 1779 at Tiegenhagen (Tujce). In 1798 living at Kalteherberge (Świerznica), near the north edge of the *Gross Werder* and the western tip of the Vistula Lagoon. Emigrated to Russia in 1804, settling at Ohrloff in Molotschna Colony. One son (Peter) stayed behind and was a wealthy grain trader in Danzig (Gdansk); in 1838 another son (Abraham) was chosen to lead the *Kleine Gemeinde* in Russia.

Johann Wiens (7) The Wienses lived near the southern point of the *Gross Werder,* between the Vistula and Nogat rivers, not far from Marienburg (Malbork) and the world's largest brick gothic castle. Johann was born in 1753 at Schoenesee (Jeziernik); he lived at Schoenau (Krasniewo), immigrated to Russia in 1804 and died at Tiege in Molotschna Colony in 1816. His grandson emigrated in 1875.

Johann Flaming (6) Born 1756 near Tragheimerweide (Przydatki), on the east side of the Vistula just south of where it splits to form the Nogat River. Earlier, the Flaming family probably lived northeast of Koenigsberg (Kalingrad) until expelled for refusal to contribute sons to King Frederick William's tall soldiers regiment. Johann moved to Russia in 1821; his grandson immigrated to the U.S. settling in Nebraska.

Hans Baltzer (6) The Baltzers fled Switzerland and then Moravia due to persecution of the Anabaptists. They may have tried to settle near Thorn

(Torun) around 1535. By 1597 they were living downriver near Montau (Matawy) and Kammerau (Osiek). Hans Baltzer was born around 1730 at Kammerau. Grandson Heinrich left Poland in 1836 as an orphaned teen, settled 1854 in Alexanderkrone, emigrated again in 1878.

Isaac Klaassen (6) Married in 1781 at Heubuden (Stogi), toward the south end of the *Gross Werder*. Lived at Gross Mausdorf (Myszewo) along the eastern edge of the *Gross Werder.* Immigrated to Russia in 1803. His grandson, Bernhard, immigrated to the U.S. in 1876.

Jacob Gerhard Dueck (5) Born 1763 near Oberfeld (Obory) into a family displaced (like the Flamings) from Tilset (Sovetsk) area. Lived at Kurzebrack (Korzeniewo). Moved to Russia in 1820; granddaughter, Margaretha, married Johann Wiens and immigrated to the U.S. in 1875.

Anna Funk (4) Born 1820 at Ober Nessau near Thorn (Torun). Her father was a farmer and minister who died when she was eight. Emigrated to Russia at age 16, married Jacob Wiens in 1841 and lived near Nikolaidorf in Molotschna Colony. Immigrated to the U.S. in 1875.

Sharon's Ancestors

Thomas Wiens (7) Born 1733 at Ellerwald (Olszanki), between the city of Elbing (Elblag) and the Nogat River. Raised his family near Marienburg (Malbork) within sight of the Castle; died in 1792. Children immigrated to Russia in 1803, settling at Altonau in Molotschna Colony. Great-great-granddaughter Justina immigrated to U.S. (Kansas) in 1874.

Nicholas Edse (6) He lived at Wengeln, just west of Lake Drausen (Druzno) and died in 1776 at Thiensdorf (Jezioro). Son Daniel and his seven children were among the group that left Russia in 1795, settling at Schoenwiese in Chortitiza Colony. Nicholas' great-grandson, Johann, led part of the family to the U.S. in 1875.

Gerhard Klassen (5) Born 180[illegible] in the city of Elbing (Elblag) and appears to have married and raised his family there. Emigrated from Prussia during the 1830s, settling at Paulsheim, in Molotschna Colony. His son, also named Gerhard, was born in Elbing in 1823, moved to Russia with his parents and then led the Klassen family to U.S. in 1875.

Appendix 4(a): Ancestors & Places in Poland

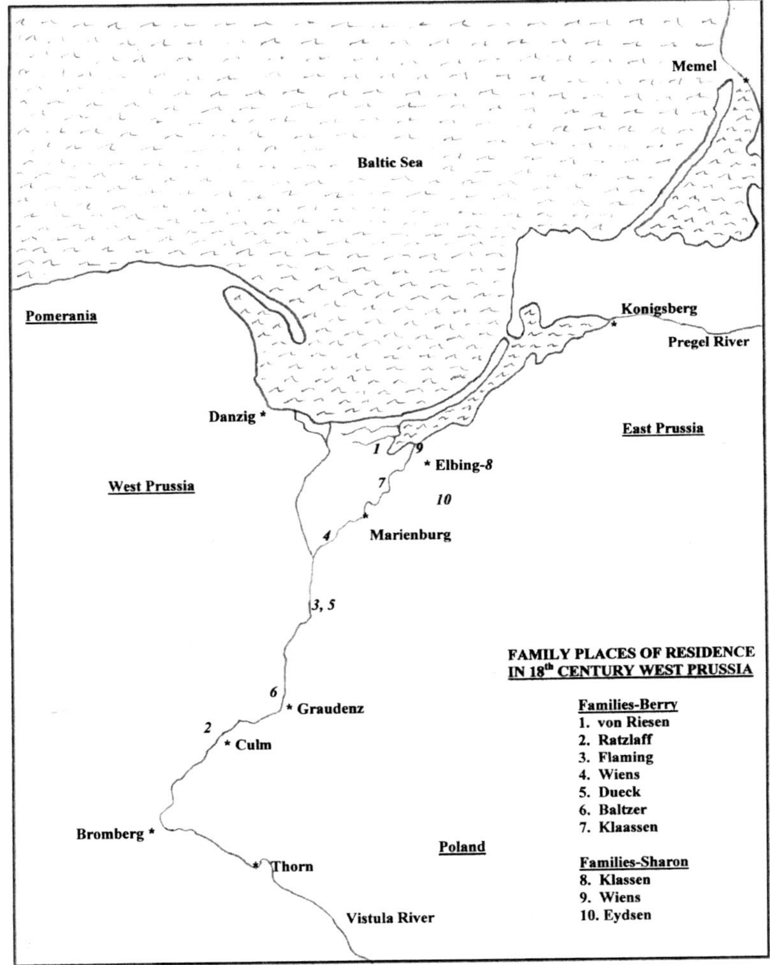

Map of major cities with their German names along the Vistula River in 18th century Prussia. Of the ten families identified, six lived on or near the Delta and four lived upriver, south of the Delta.

Appendix 4(b): Mennonite Colonies in Russia

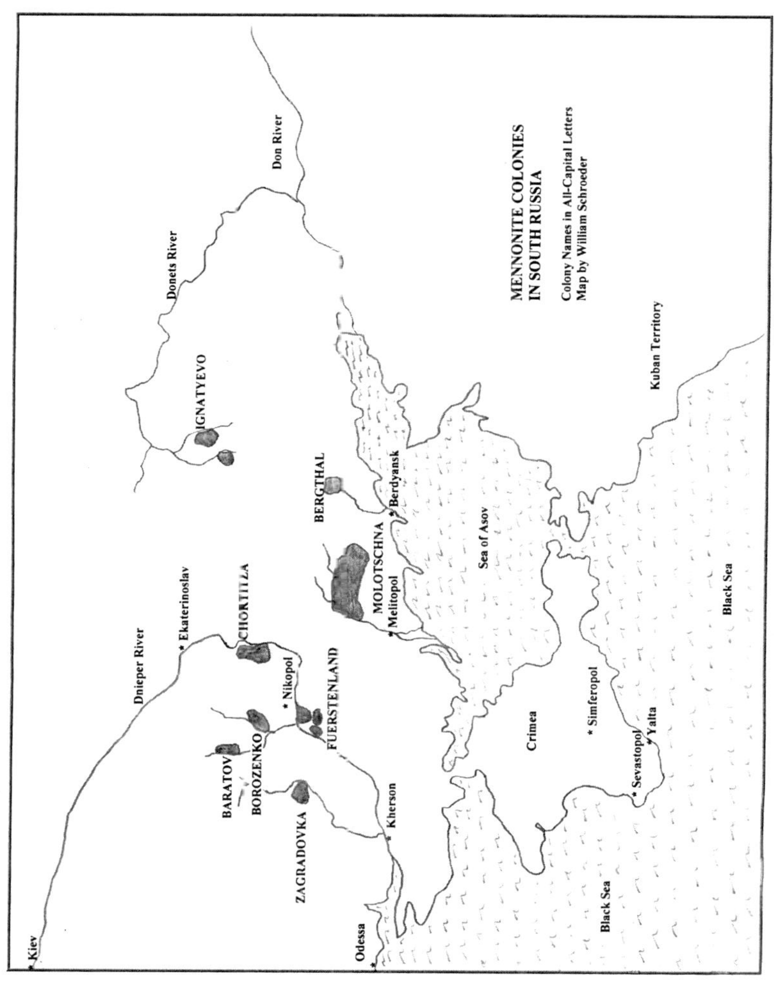

Map of southern Ukraine with locations of eight Mennonite colonies: Chortitza (1789), Molotschna (1804) , Bergthal (1836), Borozenko (1865), Fuerstenland (1865), Zagradovka (1871), Baratov (1872), and Ignatyevo (1889). See Krahn, Cornelius. "Ukraine." *Global Anabaptist Mennonite Encyclopedia Online,* 1959.

Appendix 4(c): Cottonwood County, Minnesota

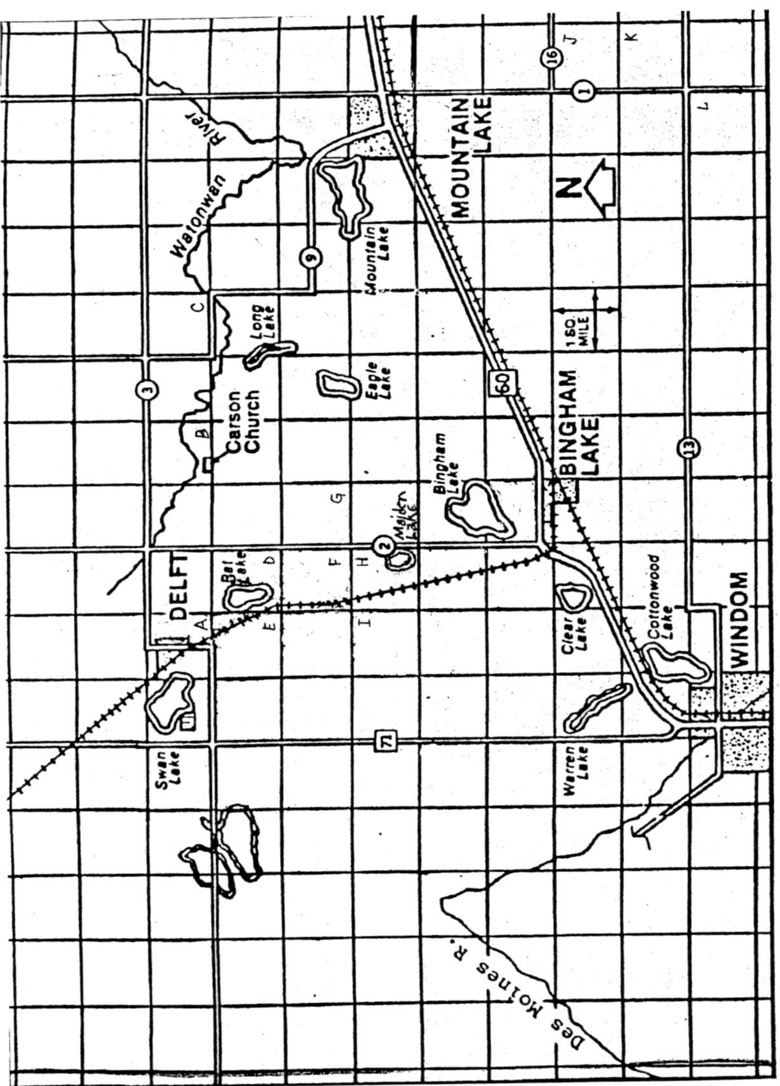

Section numbers in Carson Township: A-18; B-15; C-13; D-20; E-19; F-29; G-28; H-32; I-31. Mountain Lake Township: J-15; K-22; L-28.

Appendix 4(d): Carson Township, Minnesota

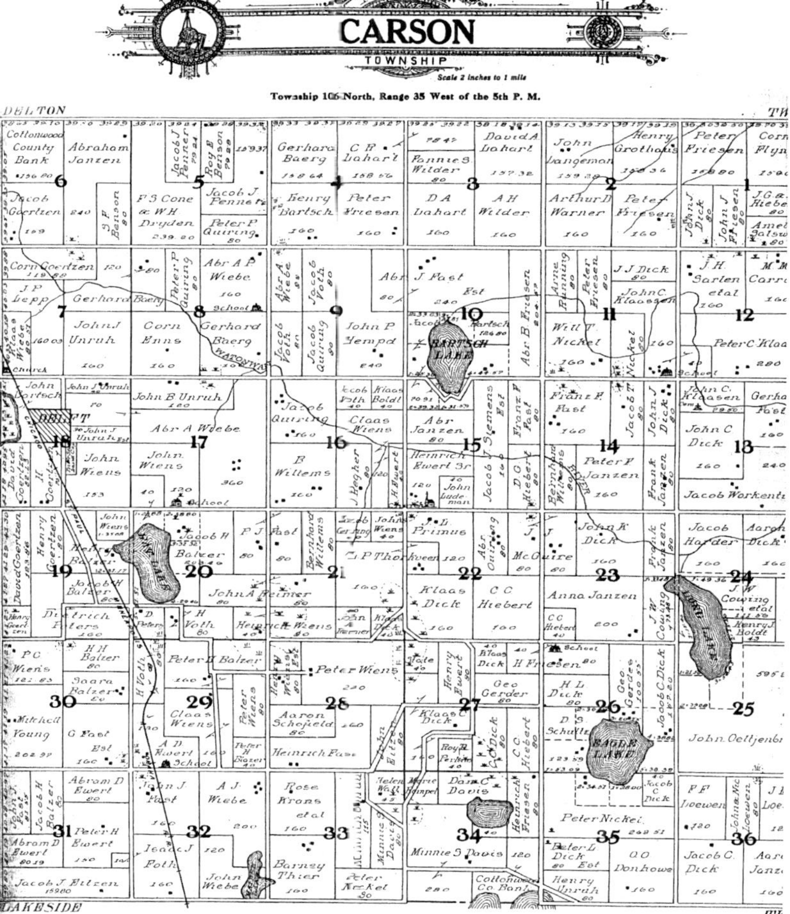

1909 map of the 36 sections of Carson Township. Wiens property is found primarily in sections 17, 18, and 28; Balzer property is found primarily in sections 19, 20 and 29; Eytzen property is found in Section 31; Wiebe property is found in Section 32.

Jacob and Maria Wiebe Eytzen with Marie and John, circa 1896.

Heinrich and Elizabeth Flaming Ratzlaff, circa 1898.

Sarah Balzer and John Wiens on their wedding day, June 8, 1911.

Johann and Margaretha Dueck Wiens with her brother, Klaas, 1911.

Jacob Balzer at age 47 upon his 1909 marriage to widow Helena Fast Flaming. Standing third from the right is his daughter, Sarah, age 20.

Wiens extended family circa 1925. In front row, Mom is 7th from left, brother Ed 8th from left and sister Charlotte 5th from left. Mom's grandpa sits in 3rd row, her mother sits in 4th, her father stands in rear.

Johann Wiebe with second wife, Maria Balzer, circa 1904. Maria Wiebe Eytzen and husband Jacob sit right; Sarah Wiebe Balzer and husband Peter sit left;. Abraham Wiebe stands third from left.

Elizabeth Voth Klassen Flaming & second husband Heinrich, c.1910. Son Abraham stands rear third from right; his wife Justina sits second from right. All eleven of Elizabeth's children appear here.

Johann Eydsen with seven of his grandchildren and daughter-in-law Maria Wiebe Eytzen on the Eytzen farm, circa 1904.

All surviving Eytzen children at Christmas gathering, circa 1958. Left-to-right stand Martha, Sara, Jake, Marie, John, Abe, Anna, Justina, Helen and Esther. Three siblings died as children.

Abraham and Justina Wiebe Klassen with children, circa 1927. Left-to-right stand Leondo, William, Elizabeth, Justina, Abe, Arnold, Sam, Amanda, and Mathilda

Will and Esther Eytzen Klassen with children Evangeline (sitting) and Sharon, Paul and Mary standing left-to-right, 1963.

Friesen family on rented farm near Jansen, Nebraska, fall 1930. Left-to-right are Helena (Lena) with firstborn Laverna Ens, Jack, Herman, George, Henry, Esther, Elizabeth, Peter and John.

Friesen family circa 1936. Front left-to-right Jack, Esther, George, Elizabeth, Lena, John; back row left-to-right Henry and wife Louise, Peter and wife Emma, Andy Ens, Susan and Herman Friesen.

A Wiens family picnic 1952. Mom & Dad are far left, second & third rows. LeRoy and Marley stand far right, front row. Mom's brothers Harold, Jack, Arnold and Ted stand right-to-left in back row. Standing first & third front left are sisters Charlotte & Marcella. Ed took photo.

John and Blondina Wiens Friesen in formal family picture from 1952. LeRoy is 12, Marlyn is 11 & Berry is nearly 4. Mom & Dad are each 34.

Will & Esther Eytzen Klassen with entire family, 1985. Sharon and daughters Amber & Emily are right of Will; Berry stands behind.

Berry & Sharon Klassen Friesen with Emily and Amber, 1994.

The last picture of Berry, LeRoy and Marlyn, taken in the fall of 1985 at the wedding of Todd Friesen and Dennette Alwine.

Friesen grandchildren together on farm after their grandmother's funeral in 1996. Left-to-right are Chad, Todd & Dennette Alwine, Amber, Emily, Benjamin, John & Sher Unruh-Friesen, Tiffany & her son, Jacob.

Esther Eytzen Klassen with family around her in celebration of her 90th birthday (April, 2005). Emily Friesen Burkholder, her husband Guy & daughter Anna were the only descendants not present at the event and were added to the lower left portion of the photo later. Their second daughter Elena was born in 2008.

Berry & Sharon Klassen Friesen on Devon moor, England, during a 2008 trip to visit Amber.

At their grandma's funeral in September, 2009, front left-to-right: Emily Friesen Burkholder, Becky Klassen Klassen, Amber Friesen, Ben Friesen; Miriam Klassen Kliewer (in middle); back left-to-right, Derek Patrick, Damon Patrick, John Unruh-Friesen, Stephen Klassen

Index of Authors